JEAN DE GRANDPRÉ

JEAN DE GRANDPRÉ
Visionary Leader

LEGACY OF A GIANT
From the Bell Telephone Company to BCE

Danielle Stanton and Hervé Anctil

McGill-Queen's University Press
Montreal & Kingston • London • Chicago

ISBN 978-0-2280-1208-5 (cloth)
ISBN 978-0-2280-1238-2 (ePDF)
ISBN 978-0-2280-1239-9 (ePUB)

Legal deposit third quarter 2022
Bibliothèque nationale du Québec

Printed in Canada on acid-free paper that is 100% ancient forest free
(100% post-consumer recycled), processed chlorine free

Funded by the Government of Canada | Financé par le gouvernement du Canada | Canada

Canada Council for the Arts | Conseil des arts du Canada

We acknowledge the support of the Canada Council for the Arts.

Nous remercions le Conseil des arts du Canada de son soutien.

Library and Archives Canada Cataloguing in Publication

Title: Jean de Grandpré, visionary leader : legacy of a giant : from the Bell Telephone Company to BCE / Danielle Stanton and Hervé Anctil.

Other titles: Jean de Grandpré, l'héritage d'un géant. English | Legacy of a giant

Names: Stanton, Danielle, author. | Anctil, Hervé, 1948- author.

Description: Translation of: Jean de Grandpré, l'héritage d'un géant. | Includes bibliographical references.

Identifiers: Canadiana (print) 20220171742 | Canadiana (ebook) 20220171785 | ISBN 9780228012085 (hardcover) | ISBN 9780228012382 (PDF) | ISBN 9780228012399 (ePUB)

Subjects: LCSH: Grandpré, A. Jean de. | LCSH: BCE Inc. – History. | LCSH: Telephone companies – Canada – History. | LCSH: Businessmen – Canada – Biography. | LCSH: Lawyers – Canada – Biography. | LCGFT: Biographies.

Classification: LCC HE8870.B45 G7313 2022 | DDC 384.6092 – dc23

This book was designed and typeset by Peggy & Co. Design in 11.5/14 Minion Pro.

CONTENTS

Milestones

JEAN DE GRANDPRÉ

The Adventure of a Lifetime, in Fast-forward

Summing up a life that extends over a century is daunting enough, and when it involves an existence as rich and eventful as Jean de Grandpré's, you need a few markers to trace the storyline. We therefore present the key moments in the great builder's life.

The early years (1921–43)

1921	Born in Montréal on 14 September.
1921–31	Childhood on Saint-Hubert Street. He is the second boy in a family of three. His two brothers, like him, will become lawyers.
1931	The family moves to Outremont.
1939	Classical studies at Collège Jean-de-Brébeuf.
1940–43	Law studies at McGill University and part-time work at the law firm Brais and Campbell.

The law years (1943-66)

1943–49	Lawyer at the firm Brais and Campbell.
1949–66	Partner at the firm Tansey, de Grandpré & de Grandpré.
1956–57	Legal counsel to the Royal Commission on Broadcasting.

1961 Appointed Queen's Counsel. The title honours lawyers who demonstrate exemplary service in the Canadian justice system.
1961–63 Member of the Barreau du Québec.
1965 Special counsel to Bell Canada. He is mandated to represent the company before the Canadian Transport Commission (then the regulatory body governing telephone services) on the sensitive issue of telephone rate review.

The Bell years (1966–83)

1966 Joins Bell Canada and appointed general counsel.
1966 Vice-president, legal department.
1968 Vice-president, administration.
1970 Vice-president, eastern region.
1972 Director and member of Bell Canada's executive committee.
1973 President, Bell Canada.
1976 Chair and CEO of Bell Canada.
1981–82 Chair of Northern Telecom's board of directors.

The BCE years (1983–89)

1983 Founder of the holding company Bell Canada Enterprises (BCE); CEO of BCE and chair of the board (until 1989).
1989 The board of directors gives him the title Founding Director and Chair Emeritus, Bell Canada Enterprises, on his departure from BCE.

Contributions, honours, and distinctions

- Jean de Grandpré has chaired the boards of the Orchestre symphonique des jeunes de Montréal and of the Mount Royal Club, and was a director at the École des hautes études commerciales de Montréal (HEC Montréal). He also served as McGill University's fifteenth chancellor from 1984 to 1991, and was appointed governor emeritus in 1992 and chancellor emeritus in 2007. He is the second chancellor in McGill's history to receive the honour (the first being Greta Chambers).

- Jean de Grandpré has sat on a number of corporate boards (including those of Bell and its subsidiaries) as chair or director: the Société Nationale d'Assurance, Royal Assurance, Sun Life Canada, the Toronto-Dominion Bank, TransCanada PipeLines, the Seagram Company Ltd, Stelco Inc., Textron, Metro One Telecommunications, Theratechnologies Inc., Chrysler Corporation and Chrysler Canada Ltd, E.I. du Pont de Nemours and Company, DuPont Canada, Cadillac Fairview, Julius Baer Canada, Montréal Trust, and United Venture Group.
- He has also sat on the international advisory boards of Goldman Sachs & Co. and Chemical Bank, both of New York, and on the board of directors of the Conference Board, which elected him associate member.
- The A. Jean de Grandpré Distinguished Speaker Series, created by Dr Chandra A. Madramootoo under the auspices of McGill University's MacDonald College, is held once a year and brings together experts in agriculture and the environment. The event was named in honour of Jean de Grandpré as a thank-you for his ardent opposition, as governor on the university's board, to the proposed transfer of McGill's agriculture faculty from the Sainte-Anne-de-Bellevue campus to the university's central location on Sherbrooke Street. His stance flew in the face of a decision by the board of governors, backed by the university's senate.
- He was a senior adviser for the creation of the Schmeelk Canada Foundation, named after the banker and great philanthropist Richard J. Schmeelk, who sought to strengthen economic and cultural ties between Québec, Canada, and the United States. The foundation's objective is to enable English-speaking students to study at French-language universities and French-speaking students to do the same at English-language ones. Each fellowship is valued at $40 thousand, an amount split over the fellowship's two years. Over the years, Jean de Grandpré would rub shoulders on

the foundation's board with a number of political figures, including Guy Saint-Pierre (a member of Robert Bourassa's Cabinet), Bill Davis (premier of Ontario), John Turner (prime minister of Canada), Raymond Garneau (also a member of Robert Bourassa's Cabinet), and many more.

- Jean de Grandpré's contribution to countless professional, educational, and community activities has earned him appointments first as officer and then as companion of the Order of Canada, and commander of the Ordre de Montréal. He is a lifetime member of the Canadian Bar Association, member emeritus of the Canadian Corporate Counsel Association and a member of the Barreau du Québec.
- In 1989, the Canadian Business Hall of Fame elected him as a member, and, four years later, the Québec Employers Council awarded him its 2013 Prix de carrière.
- Finally, to highlight his contribution to the world of telecommunications and Canadian society in general, a number of universities have bestowed honorary degrees: Université du Québec (1979), McGill University (1981), the University of Ottawa (1982), Bishop's University (1983), and Université de Montréal (1989).

Then and Now

BELL'S NINE LIVES

Bell Canada is one of the most well-known brands in the country. The brand has been in existence since 1880, the year the Bell Telephone Company of Canada was founded. The company has a long and storied history, never more marked than by Jean de Grandpré, who in the '70s and '80s pushed the company to unprecedented heights.

Bell then

When Jean de Grandpré joins Bell in 1966, the company is essentially based on telephone services and mainly serves Québec and Ontario. It also had a subsidiary, Northern Electric, that manufactures equipment for telephone companies. Its products are designed in the United States for the most part, and its commercial activities are limited almost exclusively to Canada.

By the time Jean de Grandpré leaves the company in 1989, Bell has experienced phenomenal growth. He transforms it into a holding company: Bell Canada Enterprises (BCE). Under his impetus, BCE positions itself as a key player in the telecommunications industry, not just in Canada, but on the world stage. The group also invests in other sectors and diversifies its activities. Its largest subsidiaries in the late '80s included

- Bell Canada: telephone services
- Bell–Northern Research (BNR): In the '80s, BNR laboratories are the largest independent research and development (R&D) body in the country. BNR is a veritable mine of innovation. The labs are instrumental in equipping Northern Electric (renamed Northern Telecom in 1976) to compete with the big U.S. companies on the international markets and even on their home turf.
- Northern Telecom: The company is already established as a world leader in telecommunications, especially because its leaders made the digital shift (the Digital World initiative) two or three years before everyone else.
- Bell Canada International (BCI): BCI exports Canadian genius over five continents.
- BCE Publitech (previously Tele-Direct): The company initially created to print Bell's telephone directories is now expanding its portfolio of publication and distribution projects in Canada and abroad.

BCE, also directly or indirectly, has investments in dozens of subsidiaries and affiliated companies in a range of fields.

Bell now

The Bell brand is used by the holding company BCE. The company positions itself as the country's communications leader. Its business, centred mainly in Canada, covers four main areas:

- Residential communication services, smart home services, and residential telephony services under the Bell brand in seven Canadian provinces. It also offers wireless services across the country and a wide range of business communications services.
- Multimedia services under the Bell Media brand in the sectors of traditional television (the CTV network), pay and specialty television, national radio, digital media, and outdoor advertising.

- An extensive retail network across the country under the brands Bell and The Source (consumer electronics).
- Sports and entertainment organizations, including Maple Leaf Sports & Entertainment and the Montréal Canadiens.

Jean de Grandpré at nine years old.

Roland de Grandpré (1891–1956). "He's the man I admire the most," his son Jean will say.

Collège Jean-de-Brébeuf graduating class in rhetoric, 1938–48. Jean de Grandpré (top right, middle) is class president. A certain Pierre Elliott Trudeau is vice-president (left of de Grandpré).

Receiving an honorary doctorate from the Rector Gilles Boulet of the Université du Québec in 1979. Journalist René Lecavalier and novelist Anne Hébert received the same honour.

In 1987, he is admitted to the Academy of Great Montréalers, alongside actor Jean Duceppe and neuropsychologist Brenda Milner.

Saudi Arabia celebrates historic event

Saudi Arabia calls on Bell to modernize and develop its telecommunications network. Jean de Grandpré spearheads the international breakthrough. Above, he is received by the Saudi communications minister Dr Alawi Darweesh Kayal in 1987.

In 1989, Jean de Grandpré and Rowland C. Frazee co-chaired the Montreal Children's Hospital's campaign "Ensemble pour nos enfants" ("Together for Our Children"). They raised over $40 million.

Orland Tropea, Jean de Grandpré's right-hand man at Bell.

Former prime minister Pierre Elliott Trudeau, who was a classmate of the future Bell CEO. Behind, his friend Marcel Casavant.

Jean de Grandpré made numerous business trips to Japan.

Former prime minister Jean Chrétien at the inauguration of the de Grandpré Communications Centre at the Montreal Neurological Institute-Hospital.

Bob Eaton (left), former chair of Chrysler, alongside Malcolm Stamper (Boeing), Robert Lanigan (Owens-Illinois), and Jean de Grandpré.

As director of Textron, which controlled Bell Helicopter, Jean de Grandpré thanks and congratulates employees who have just finished building the one thousandth helicopter.

Two great leaders: Ted Newall, CEO of DuPont Canada, and Jean de Grandpré.

Opening of the de Grandpré Communications Centre at the Montréal Neurological Institute-Hospital in 2000, thanks to a donation from Jean de Grandpré and his family.

Chancellor Emeritus of McGill University in 2007 with his daughter Lili.

From top to bottom: The Papillon Foundation camp cafeteria (Bistro Chez Hélène) and gymnasium (Chez François).

The work of a L'Amitient protégé: *The Essence of the Golden-Crowned Kinglet*, by Jérôme Vermette.

Relaxing at home.

Wonderful memory of a family gathering. Jean de Grandpré surrounded by his children (left to right) Lili, Suzanne, François, and Loulou (Louise).

With his wife Hélène. "Without her, I could never have had this career," says Jean de Grandpré.

JEAN DE GRANDPRÉ

Introduction

BECOMING SOMEBODY

On the table in the vast living room with light wood panelling lie the work documents: everything is all set for the interview. Efficiency is clearly hard-wired in Jean de Grandpré's DNA.

"Come in!" His smile is warm, his manner friendly, but his tone is firm and his gaze, direct and unflinching. It only takes two words when he lets us in and already we know there's an innate authority about Jean de Grandpré that cannot be denied nor explained – and that comes from within. An authority that leaders have in common. Add to that keen intelligence, sound judgment, and an iron will, and you have the tools that helped Jean de Grandpré build an empire: the Bell empire.

"Would you rather we meet at home or in my office?" he had asked the day before. Yes, Jean de Grandpré still has an office on the nineteenth floor of the Bell Canada Tower on Beaver Hall Hill, where he still goes regularly. At the age of ninety-eight, his career is over, but Bell has never left him, especially as the retired-in-slippers-by-the-fire look doesn't particularly suit him!

An avid daily rider of his stationary bicycle, the man stays active, physically and intellectually. He is also actively involved in a camp for children with disabilities, so much so that Jean Duchesneau, general manager of the Papillon Foundation heading the charitable project, remarks, "At first, I hesitated to tell him about the occasional hiccups we had to avoid worrying him. That was a mistake.

I soon understood that the opposite was true: he loved trying to find ways around obstacles."

Old photos show a man with an impressive physique. Today, dressed in a well-cut sports shirt and matching pants, the man before us is slim and elegant. His posture is straight, his bearing imposing, and his energy palpable. Everything about Jean de Grandpré belies his age, including his phenomenal memory. And his laugh … the laugh of a child proud of his achievements. Achievements? He's had quite a few.

Jean de Grandpré is an extraordinary person. It runs in the family. His father, Roland, a self-taught man, was known as one of the most brilliant insurance experts in Canada (See sidebar It Runs in the Family, page 12). Jean remembers what he was taught: "It's possible for a francophone to succeed in business in an anglophone world. And being interested in money isn't a sin." An opinion Jean de Grandpré's mother – a strong, determined woman – heartily shared.

With his well-chosen words, perfect syntax, and unhesitating delivery, Jean de Grandpré's French is impeccable. For a moment, you forget that from the time he started studying at McGill University, he lived his life primarily in English. "I lived on both sides of the fence: in French at home and usually in English outside."

And the term Québecer? He prefers Canadian.

> I love Québec; it's near and dear to me. But I don't define myself as that, nor, for that matter, as French-Canadian, a term that in my opinion suggests detachment, closing in. I'm a Canadian, period.

Hard not to think otherwise with his background and career. One thing is for sure, the dual cultural identity that grounds Jean de Grandpré's personality is similar to that of Pierre Elliott Trudeau, one of his classmates at Collège Jean-de-Brébeuf, a man whose path he would cross in countless circumstances throughout his life.

Like Canada's former prime minister, Jean de Grandpré could have gone into politics. He was actually approached to do so more than once, but he always declined the offer. "My wife made it clear:

'Jean, if you go into politics, I'm getting a divorce.' Her decision was final."

And so it was. But even if there had been no affectionate warning, could de Grandpré have moved serenely into the cryptic world of politics – a man who had been allergic to any form of regimentation all his life? The response is emphatic: "Not for one minute!"

The man likes to have leeway. He likes a clear horizon – literally and figuratively. "When I left my office at Bell at the end of the day, all my dossiers had been filed or sent on to whomever had to deal with them. There was absolutely nothing left on my desk." For Jean de Grandpré, clarity is a sacred virtue, the reflection of a rigorous work ethic.

Pragmatic. That's what he is. So it's no surprise to learn that, despite being chief executive officer (CEO), he preferred to make his phone calls himself rather than ask his secretary, as every other CEO did. "It was so much faster and simpler! When I'm at the office, I still work like that."

"An Uncomplicated Man" was the title one magazine gave to an article about him. True, yet oversimplified at the same time. Indeed, de Grandpré doesn't bother with digressions and clever displays. But don't let appearances fool you. If he always manages to go straight to the point, it's because he has a rare talent: he knows how to break down the most sophisticated concepts to make them digestible and understandable to all, a trademark that earned him the nickname the "Simplifier."

Uncomplicated, but nevertheless complex, Jean de Grandpré is not without paradox. Who would have thought that a man who worked in a business community so deeply attached to convention would never sign an employment contract with Bell? His salary was set by the executive compensation committee. The president would convey the decision to him and he would accept it, without negotiation. "I wanted to be free to leave at any time if it no longer worked out," he explains. "And I wanted Bell's senior management to enjoy the same latitude." Jean de Grandpré is no rebellious delinquent, but can certainly be bold when he wants to be. This particular approach will nevertheless serve him well.

> When I joined the company, I didn't ask for anything in exchange for my twenty-one years of experience as a lawyer. But when I retired, I was told that the period would be taken into account when they determined the amount of my pension. A gift from heaven!

The "Architect" and the "Tactician" are other nicknames for the man who tackles problems like no one else – in a logical, almost mathematical, way. The "Strategist," they sometimes add, in recognition of his skills at achieving his ends. "My children sometimes compare me – albeit kindly – to Machiavelli's prince, the strategist par excellence."

Jean de Grandpré, gives himself another title: "I'm stubborn, yes; truly pigheaded, as we say at home! When I think I'm right, I don't give in: I'm ready to fight till the end." He is described as having the instinct of a fighter and the wisdom of a head of state. An explosive combination. Others have accused him of being tough: "If I have been on occasion, it was to defend the interests of the company and protect the people who work there."

Most of the people who have rubbed shoulders with Jean de Grandpré describe him as a civilized, affable, and courteous man. You have no trouble believing them, judging by the impressive network of acquaintances and friends he developed in his life. Politics, business – Jean de Grandpré was on a first-name basis with key players in every sphere across the country and internationally. His impressive ability to connect with people played a decisive role in his career.

Jean de Grandpré is a worker to the bone. But in his time off he enjoys reading, biographies most of all. "I especially like biographies of leaders. I think I've read the biographies of all the Canadian prime ministers and American presidents." Of all of them, George H.W. Bush, whom he has met personally, particularly inspires him. "He commands my admiration. He was a gentleman; he respected everyone. Most of all, he had solid experience and knew where he was going." Just like Jean de Grandpré.

The walls of his apartment are adorned with paintings – figurative works. Abstract art holds little interest for de Grandpré. Neither contemplative, nor meditative, he's more comfortable with the concrete and with action. "You've got to move forward."

> The worst decision is the one you don't make. If there's a decision to make, it means something isn't working. You have to act: you have a 50 per cent chance of getting it right and a 50 per cent chance of getting it wrong. But if you don't do anything, you have a 100 per cent chance of seeing things turn out badly! All my life, I've been giving the same advice: Make the damn decision!

Success belongs to those who know how to bring about change: "Movement is the only way to avoid atrophy." That said, the decisions Jean de Grandpré made weren't always the right ones. He is the first to admit it. "Having the humility to recognize your mistakes is an important value, in my eyes. Above all, you can't be someone you're not."

The circumstances of his life led the lawyer to where he was at Bell, where he excelled. But with the cards he was dealt, he would have succeeded anywhere. The young man whose motto was "Be somebody" achieved his goal.

BELL AND CANADA: CROSSED DESTINIES

For Jean de Grandpré, the destinies of Canada and Bell are inextricably linked. What's good for Bell is good for Canada: he would make this his credo.

He speaks of the connection for the first time in 1965 before he had even joined Bell, when he was defending the company on the delicate matter of rates.

> Good communications are essential to ... business if the latter wishes to operate swiftly and efficiently. Without rapid transmission of information ... Canadian business will not be in a position to match the competition of foreign exporters, and we know from history that exports are at the source of growth of the Canadian economy. Bell will not be in a position to play its role in the development of the country if its construction program is curtailed by lack of funds.[1]

These crossed destinies will be mentioned again, on a patriotic note this time, in Bell's 1974 annual report.

> Canadians are privileged among the peoples of the world. It is an age when social and economic uncertainties are common to all nations. But Canada is more tranquil than most and can rely on an unusual depth of human and material resources. This land is strong because of its people, its institutions, and its will to meet the challenges of our times. The telecommunications industry has remarkably developed over the years to better meet the needs of the population of such a vast country. The achievements of the industry and of your company are simply a prologue to a promising future. Canada will grow and Canadians will prosper in this quarter century, perhaps as never before. With Bell Canada often leading, never trailing, telecommunications will develop rapidly.

1 Surtees, *Pa Bell*, 52.

De Grandpré will again highlight the osmosis between Bell and Canada in 1983 to justify the creation of the BCE holding company:

> This reorganization is essential to continue what we have been trying to do for ten years … there is no doubt in my mind that the reorganization is something that must be approved because it is of paramount importance for Canada. It's a way of flying the Canadian flag, if you like, all over the world.[2]

His attachment to his country is deep, but it doesn't prevent Jean de Grandpré from defining himself as an internationalist, one determined not to let any border stand in his way. And he is quick to reproach Canada for its lack of enthusiasm toward big companies, such as Bell, which he interprets as a reflexive insularity. "Thinking big," he says, "doesn't seem to be a Canadian virtue."

2 Surtees, *Pa Bell*, 303.

1

HEAD OF THE CLASS

Jean de Grandpré's career is built on a solid foundation, having had attentive parents and highly qualified teachers, along with his extraordinary intelligence and iron will added to the mix. The only thing left to add is a touch of luck.

> My mother always said, "Jean wasn't just born with a horseshoe around his neck; he had a golden horseshoe!"

And, as Jean de Grandpré's life most emphatically attests, Aline Magnan was right.

But, meanwhile, the little guy has problems. With fragile health, looking somewhat thin, and wearing nerdy glasses, he attracts more than his fair share of mockery from the neighbourhood kids.

One fine September morning in 1927, Jean is six and it is his first day at the Sœurs de la Providence kindergarten on Saint-Denis Street, close to where he lives on Saint-Hubert Street. And yet, because it is very hot, Aline decides it is more appropriate to put him in shorts rather than pants as the rules specify. "After all, Saint John the Baptist bared his knees!" she argues. "If the principal objects, well, you'll just have to go to the Jewish school next door." What a mistake! Children are often cruel, and the hilarity caused by his shorts is something the child will never forget. He is hurt.

He takes a blow. But whereas another person would settle for staggering under it, Jean de Grandpré learns a life lesson: better to lead than to be led.

At home, life is rosy. Jean, his older brother, Louis-Philippe, and the baby of the family, Pierre, live happily, dividing their time between roller skating, lacrosse, and hockey. And the bird game.

> We used a modified broom handle to hit a small stick called a "bird" because of the way it flew. This game, which was also called "the stick game," was very popular in my youth.

Kids will be kids. Naturally Jean and his friends sometimes get up to mischief. Many of their shenanigans will even have the honour of being immortalized in a comic strip in *La Presse* by journalist Fernand Roby, a neighbour of the de Grandpré family.

The Great Depression hits in 1929. Although his salary is reduced by a third, Roland de Grandpré – one of the most brilliant Canadian insurance company managers of his day, at a time when Montréal is the commercial and financial capital of the country – will shelter his family from the storm. Is it any wonder? Roland is a fighter, as his meteoric rise attests, and a father who would be a decisive example for his son. "He's the man I admire most."

As proof things are going well, the family moves to the posh neighbourhood of Outremont in 1931 to live in the house Roland had built on Beloeil Avenue. It is awash with light: "Papa adored light! I inherited that love." In Jean de Grandpré's current apartment at the top of a Montréal tower, the sun streams through every window, literally flooding the space. Jean de Grandpré is a man of clarity, literally and figuratively.

If Roland runs a tight ship outside, at home, it is undeniably Aline who holds the rudder. Three words guide her: love, work, and discipline.

This forceful woman, who is taller than her husband, is known for her outspokenness, a trait inherited by Jean. Aline has strong opinions about everything! "Maman did not hesitate to express her opinion that a father's contribution to a child's education was never more than five per cent of the total."

One thing is certain, the education of her three sons is very important to her. Demanding? Yes. But without being rigid and a stickler for the rules. "Once in a while she let me play in the snow instead of study. She would say, 'Go ahead, you won't be able to do it when you're 40.' " A scenario that was probably unusual at the time.

More exceptionally still, Aline, the strong woman that she is, is quick to decide that part of her sons's elementary education will be provided at home. It is all a matter of learning faster, she decided.

IT RUNS IN THE FAMILY

Meteoric: There's no better word to sum up the rise of Jean's father, Roland de Grandpré. At the time of his death, in 1956, he is one of Canada's foremost insurance authorities. You would never have guessed that fifty years earlier, when, in 1906, fifteen-year-old Roland decides to leave his birthplace of New England to return to the land of his ancestors, Québec.

Yes, oddly enough, Jean de Grandpré's father is an American. After studies in medicine, Louis-Philippe, Jean's grandfather, chooses to settle in New England, partly for the milder climate, but most of all to flee – as many of his compatriots did – the harsh economic climate that then dims prospects in Québec. He moves to Fall River, Massachusetts, where a Québec community is already established, and in 1887 marries a Québecer, Marie-Louise Beaudry. Roland is born in 1891 on 4 July, American Independence Day.

Having finished his studies at Classical High in Manchester, Roland decides to return to his roots. He arrives in Montréal and continues his studies at the Commercial and Technical High School. He teaches himself French with Augé's *Grammaire* until he is perfectly bilingual.

He finds his first job in 1908 as an office boy at Evans & Johnson, a small insurance agency in Montréal. He proceeds to work in a number of different companies in the field, slowly climbing the ladder, still with no training in actuarial science or administration. And once again, as he did with French, he learns them on his own. "My father was the only person I know who had read the insurance dictionary from cover to cover," says Jean. At thirty, the self-learner becomes manager for Canada of two U.S.-based companies: the New Hampshire Fire Insurance Company and the Granite State Fire Insurance Company, before becoming, a few years later, the president of the Canadian Underwriters Association (CUA) and the Dominion Board of Insurance Underwriters.

Roland de Grandpré earns his professional laurels by dint of hard work. He has no hobbies or pastimes, and his only vice is chocolate. He is said to eat up to five pounds a week. But as far as everything else is concerned, Roland de Grandpré is diligence itself, working twelve hours a day, and often agreeing to do overtime so that Aline, who married him in 1916, and their three sons can live in comfort.

This relentless worker has only one wish: to do everything in his power to ensure his children climb the social ladder and achieve bigger things than he has. He will always be an example to Jean and his brothers. Work and discipline go hand in hand with success. Roland also passes on to his sons his guilt-free attitude toward money. Contrary to what the Catholic Church then preaches, he thinks it legitimate and respectable to aspire to financial success.

On his death, in 1956, the CUA magazine editorializes, "Roland de Grandpré worked hard and tirelessly. No task was too difficult for him; he performed each with admirable determination and skill. His colleagues held him in very high esteem." The *Chronicle*, too, approves, recalling that when he was president of the CUA, he had insisted on setting up a translation department so that all of the association's documentation could be available in both French and English. From a man who had spent so much energy teaching himself French when he arrived in the country, it was a perfectly logical decision.

Roland de Grandpré's influence over his son's personal and professional life is undeniable: "When I look at my reflection in the mirror, it's my father I see. My whole life I've tried to be like him."

> I learned reading, writing, adding, and subtracting – all the preparatory year topics – at home. So I went into first grade right away. I also skipped second grade and went directly into third because my mother thought that most of the second-year content was just a recap of the first.

Aline will be actively involved in his education.

> I remember, like it was yesterday, the ingenious way she illustrated the equator and the solar system. An orange represented the Earth, and an elastic around its middle symbolized the equator. A knitting needle indicated the Earth's axis.

As soon as he can read fluently, young Jean tears through the twelve volumes of *The Children's Encyclopedia*, then does the same with Augé's *Grammaire* – the one his father used to learn how to write French correctly – and a pile of novels by the Comtesse de Ségur.

Exceptional son, exceptional mother. For her three sons, Aline Magnan has big, very big, ambitions: "A judge in the Supreme Court, a prime minister, and a pope, that's what she wanted for us. Nothing less. In my mother's dreams, our future was all mapped out."

His mother, for whom he still holds an undying affection, will be a beacon for him: "She was an extraordinary woman." She won't be the only one; other women in his life will soon play a decisive role.

Discipline, discipline, discipline

> Throughout my entire career, I've had to express myself in public. If I've been able to defend myself as an orator, it's primarily because of my elementary school teachers. These invaluable women knew the importance of speaking correctly, with flawless diction. How many people today seem to have forgotten that to communicate properly you have to open your mouth and ar-ti-cu-late!

The nuns will instill in him an enduring legacy: the value of discipline, an asset that Jean de Grandpré will draw from again and again. He does not deviate: without discipline, without a framework, success is not possible. And that goes for everything.

> "In Japan, all the school children wear uniforms," he gives as an example at a meeting one day. "How can you impart a sense of discipline and the importance of dressing well when the teacher is teaching in a T-shirt and jeans?"

"What's worth doing is worth doing well." Jean de Grandpré adopts the famous adage prominently displayed on the wall of the family home. Discipline, a sense of duty, and a desire to succeed – the young man is primed for the next chapter in the story: his entry into the select Collège Jean-de-Brébeuf.

The objective at Brébeuf is clear: to educate the *crème de la crème*. The elite. The leaders of tomorrow. A plan that suits Jean's parents to a T. School, family – everything is falling into place. His destiny awaits.

The snobs

"Jean had a love for work well done, the courage of his convictions, and the respect of his colleagues. Even if, at times, we found him overly studious,"[1] confesses Gilles Lamontagne, former mayor of Québec City, former federal minister, and a friend of Jean de Grandpré in his college years. The man in question disowns an aura of model student.

"I wasn't a maniac! I studied, yes, but I did a lot of other things." Theatre is one. He plays priest and martyr Jean de Brébeuf in the play *L'âme huronne*. He also takes great delight in participating, alongside colleague Albert Gadbois (future member of the Canadian Pacific legal team), in humorous French debates that pit the law students of McGill against their counterparts at the Université de Montréal. These debates are poetically named *Clair de lune et clair de l'autre ou l'amour en rumble seat*[2] (Plain language from one person to the next, or love in the rumble seat). These wildly popular evenings, which take place at the École du Plateau, raise funds for the end-of-year prom. Did he bring the audience to its feet at these performances? Quite possibly. Performing, for the future lawyer, is second nature.

In the Jesuit-run school, Jean de Grandpré finds another role to his taste. Rigorous, logical, gifted with exceptional analytical skills, the young man is an excellent debater, so much so they nickname him the "Rhetorician." No wonder: with the strong showing of lawyers in his family tree, the art of arguing and defending a case is hard-wired in his DNA.

Jean de Grandpré finds this composite profile of pride, eloquence, and keen intelligence in a colleague: Pierre Elliott Trudeau, the

1 Bantey, "Un homme pas compliqué," 25.
2 Rumble seat: an uncovered folding seat in the rear of a car. (*Canadian Oxford Dictionary* 2 ed.)

future prime minister of Canada. Unsurprisingly, both are among the founders, with Father Bernier, of a select club: the Académie arts-sciences de Brébeuf. De Grandpré will be its first president; Trudeau, the secretary.

The académie's raison d'être is clearly defined: To create an elite group of distinguished young people, gifted with good general culture, who know how to express themselves with ease, accuracy, and elegance. To prepare these young people to later constitute the country's elite. The college's motto *Viam veritatis elegi* (I have chosen the way of the truth) encapsulates its high aspirations. Happily, its members know how to make fun of themselves, renaming their club "The Snobs," a nickname that amuses de Grandpré to this day.

> Pierre Trudeau was reproached for being a snob. He really wasn't all that much of one. He was much more quick-witted than me. However, I might have had a little more judgment than him! Intelligence is shaped by two things: intellect and judgment. Ideally, you should have both.

Both young men have affinities, despite their different origins. Like many students at Brébeuf, Pierre Elliott Trudeau comes from old money. Jean de Grandpré, on the other hand, is the son of a self-made man. Yet he has a priceless gift: natural authority. "Jean didn't have to push and shove to get himself noticed," recalls Gilles Lamontagne. "As soon as he entered the room, you knew he was there."[3] The future Bell CEO has another ace up his sleeve. The man who will be president of his conventum – the sixth year of the eight-year classical bachelor of arts program (Trudeau will be vice-president) – is known for his exceptional ability to achieve consensus. Jean de Grandpré has the charisma of a leader.

In the tenth-anniversary class reunion yearbook, his former classmates will recall "his imposing bearing, his amiable and cheerful personality ... his friendship for all, his understated and persuasive eloquence, and his common sense." And will conclude, "he's still the thoughtful, cheerful, and just plain nice guy we always knew."

---

3 Bantey, "Un homme pas compliqué," 25.

His teachers are just as positive in their opinions: "I am absolutely certain this young man will not disappoint," Brébeuf prefect Father Donat Boutin predicted as early as 1940. "His personality is taking shape every day and bodes great success."

One thing is certain, Jean de Grandpré is eager to learn. Humanities, history, the arts – he accumulates every bit of knowledge his talented professors impart. His mind opens: "I became aware that the world was a big place. And that there were many things to do in it."

This high-quality education comes with a significant benefit: many of his colleagues will later end up in key positions in every sphere of society. At Brébeuf, Jean de Grandpré begins to build his future network of influence. A web he will continue to weave – only this time in English – during his studies at McGill University.

Until then, Jean never had an English-speaking friend. It doesn't matter! For him, choosing McGill is a no-brainer.

> My brother Louis-Philippe had done law there. But most importantly, my father was absolutely determined that I should become perfectly bilingual so that I could make a career worthy of the name. He strongly encouraged me in my choice. And he was right.

In Jean de Grandpré's life, this immersion into a new world will be decisive: "At home, we spoke French. But otherwise, my professional life was mainly in English."

With great distinction!

Become a doctor like his grandfather? Or why not a tennis champ? Before taking up law at university, the young de Grandpré ponders other avenues. He has a genuine talent for tennis, a sport he has played since he was nine. His parents, however, are less than thrilled at the prospect of a tennis player's life, and he drops the idea. As for medicine, after reading the curriculum, any calling he might have had quickly fades: "The sight of blood and organs, wasn't, let us say, much of a draw." Law wins the day.

In the beginning, he is attracted to international law. He already sees himself entering the Ministry of Foreign Affairs, becoming an ambassador perhaps, and seeing the world. But in 1942, between his second and third year at university, a number of ambassadors are appointed by the government. He becomes disillusioned: "All political appointments." The prospect of playing second fiddle so that he could make an inexperienced ambassador look good held little appeal. He takes on a new tack: he opts for civil law.

When he starts at McGill, he speaks English, of course, but his vocabulary is limited. "It was so bad that in the first year I wrote my exams in French." Out of thirty students, Jean de Grandpré is one of only two francophones – a situation, he maintains, that never puts him at a disadvantage: "I never experienced the slightest discrimination, not even for an instant." The facts speak for themselves: in October, barely two months after the semester began, Jean de Grandpré is elected president of the class.

When asked to explain this feat, he simply says, "All my life, people have said that I have the bearing of a leader. Maybe they have a point." Jean de Grandpré is perfectly aware of this quality, but boastfulness isn't his style. "Boasting is a flaw I despise the most."

He would nevertheless have much to show off about. In his second year, he is named president of the law faculty students, and then faculty delegate to the university's student council, duties that will in no way prevent him from keeping up with his studies.

"Le succès à McGill de M. J. de Grandpré" ("Mr J. de Grandpré's Success at McGill") is the headline of an article in *La Presse* in 1941, while *La Patrie* publishes a report entitled "Les nôtres à l'honneur" ("Home Town Kids Make Good"), and for good reason. Coming first in civil law and Roman law, second in accounting and criminal law, and third in international law, Jean de Grandpré caps his first year in the faculty by becoming the first francophone at McGill to win the Adolphe-Mailhot Memorial Prize awarded by the Barreau du Québec.

The next year he does it again, taking the Alexander Morris Exhibition Prize for being first in class. And to complete his hat trick, he ends his bachelor of civil law with first-class honours and wins the Elizabeth Torrance Gold Medal for coming in first, once again, in his final exams. Not to mention the Young Bar Association of Montréal prize for the highest marks in the civil proceedings exams, and the Montréal Bar Association prize for his brilliant results in commercial law.

Clearly Jean de Grandpré is gifted. Armed with these credentials, he sets himself a life goal. At McGill, he appropriates the motto from his class at Brébeuf, *Being somebody*, and personalizes it: *Be somebody*.

A consuming ambition?

> I wanted to accomplish something that was above the average, that's true. But not out of sheer vanity. Simply because, if you really want to succeed at something, you have to become somebody. Well, I felt that a country such as ours needed leaders.

He aspires to become one.

But at the time, it is soldiers that Canada needs. The country is at war, conscription has begun. As long as they pass their exams, Jean de Grandpré and his peers are exempt from going to the front. It is an incentive to excel, naturally, but also, as they are reminded by the university authorities, a privilege: "We had a great debt to pay to society."

The Second World War has an influence of another kind on his career. McGill offers him a scholarship to continue his studies in the United States – a proposal he declines, specifically on his father's advice. "At the time, the United States was wholly engaged in the war effort, and in this context certain faculties, such as law, were considered non-essential. Also, as I had already started law practice, returning to full-time studies appealed to me less. I have never regretted my decision."

During his studies, Jean de Grandpré starts an internship with the Honourable Philippe Brais, one of the highest-profile lawyers in Canada, "an extraordinary legal expert and an extraordinary man."

When Jean de Grandpré turns eighteen he is given his first mandate: a coroner's investigation. "I didn't even know where the coroner's office was. Then – and I was still a student – I had to present several petitions and motions in court. Did I violate the act respecting the Barreau du Québec? Good gracious, I don't know."

A REMARKABLE ANCESTRY

The de Grandpré family is one of the oldest in Québec. In 1662, an ancestor named Charles Duteau, a native of Rouen, France, sets foot in Batiscan, in the Mauricie region, north-east of Trois-Rivières. His grandson Jacques, born in 1724, is the first to append "de Grandpré" to his name.

No one knows the exact reason for the addition, but one thing is certain, says Jean de Grandpré: "Contrary to what you may think, the particle 'de' has nothing to do with a title." If Jean de Grandpré has any blue blood in his veins, it's due to his mother, Aline Magnan. Her ancestor, Guillaume de Lorimier, who arrives on these shores in 1685, is the son of a French seigneur in Orléans.

Jean de Grandpré's grandfather, Louis-Philippe, leads an active life. Having settled in the United States after his medical studies, he goes to France to do postdoctoral research in a new field: infectious diseases and public health. Back in Montréal, he is put in charge of the city's public health department before returning to live in New England. His career is a thousand miles away from a lawyer's. And yet ...

> My grandfather was probably a frustrated lawyer. The proof? When he died, his holograph will was so complex that it was impossible to find two law firms in Montréal that could agree on his true intentions.

Jean de Grandpré owes his legal bent more to his maternal great-grandfather, Charles C. de Lorimier. As a superior court judge, he oversees the creation of one of the first major law texts in Québec, *La bibliothèque du Code civil de la province de Québec.* Begun in 1871 and completed in 1890, this twenty-one-volume treatise compiles all the references on which the Civil Code is based at the time. Another de Lorimier is remembered for an entirely different feat.

François-Marie-Thomas Chevalier de Lorimier and his younger brother Jean-Baptiste (father of Charles) marry two sisters, Henriette and Rachel Cadieux. Both men are involved in the

Patriots' War. After the failure of the Battle of Saint-Eustache in 1837, they flee to the United States. Although Jean-Baptiste remains there until 1843, his brother returns to Québec to continue the fight. Chevalier de Lorimier is one of the twelve patriots hanged by the British for having participated in the Lower Canada Rebellions led by Louis-Joseph Papineau in 1837 and 1838.

Worth mentioning, too, is Jean de Grandpré's maternal grandfather, Arthur Magnan, who marries Ada de Lorimier, daughter of Charles-Chamilly, born in Dubuque, Iowa, in 1842. Arthur is a tax collector for the City of Montréal. As an interesting historical footnote, Arthur's father, Louis-Adolphe Magnan, is the son-in-law of a certain Martine Dorothée Phineas, daughter of Isaac Heinemann Phineas, one of the first Jews to arrive in Canada. "So I have a few drops of Jewish blood too!"

And, for good measure, there's La Vérendrye, the first European explorer to see the Rocky Mountains, yet another of de Grandpré's famous ancestors. Clearly, the urge to break new ground runs in the family.

Explorer, Jew, patriot, and eminent jurist. When Jean de Grandpré says, "I have a very special ancestry," he isn't kidding.

It isn't long before Philippe Brais sees the young man's potential, going so far as to make him his spiritual son and even lending him his splendid Ford convertible on occasion to get to class. "That man really fast-tracked my career," de Grandpré acknowledges. With his studies complete, Jean de Grandpré starts full time at Brais and Campbell, which becomes Brais, de Grandpré in 1946. He will not go to war, but epic battles – the legal kind – are ahead. Let the battles begin.

2

The Law Years (1943–66)

A FLYING START

Jean de Grandpré would practise law for twenty-three years, as many years as he would spend at Bell. He would work in three sectors: insurance law, labour relations, and administrative law, and gain a wealth of experience that would make him one of the most skilful managers Canada has ever known.

Jean de Grandpré barely begins his practice when he is plunged into the heart of two affairs that prove deeply embarrassing for the Canadian government of the time: the Gouzenko Affair, named after a Russian spy who sought political asylum in Canada in September 1945, only weeks after the end of the Second World War; and the saga of the Polish National Treasures. The stories date back to the darkest moments of the Cold War and anti-Communist hysteria. It is a time when the Soviet Union and the United States are asserting their influence over the world, then divided into two blocks, the East and the West. The split will endure until the fall of the Berlin Wall in 1989.

Jean de Grandpré is only twenty-four when the Gouzenko Affair breaks out. He has just joined the firm of Philippe Brais. The firm will play a central role in the story, and the young recruit will be closely associated with it. These are the facts:

The Gouzenko Affair

Igor Gouzenko is hired by the Soviet Embassy in Canada when it is created in 1942, and tasked with coding the secret messages that Moscow sends to Canadian spies. Captivated by Canada's individual freedoms, Gouzenko makes the decision to expose the spies to the Canadian government in September 1945 at the end of the war.

At first, Ottawa doesn't take him seriously. Prime Minister Mackenzie King is seeking to avoid confrontation with the USSR, Canada's ally in the Second World War. Moscow, for its part, is demanding that Canada's Department of External Affairs arrest the criminal. Ultimately, Ottawa decides to grant him political asylum. Until his death, in June 1982, Gouzenko will live the life of a recluse for fear of assassination.

Gouzenko's revelations and the hundreds of documents he has purloined are instrumental in dismantling a spy ring that branches throughout Canada and into Great Britain and the United States. At the head of the ring is member of Parliament Fred Rose (from his real surname Rosenberg). Rose is the first and only member of the Communist Party to be elected to the House of Commons. He is arrested in March 1946 and accused of espionage. He will serve a six-year prison sentence and then go into exile in Poland, his country of origin, where he will end his days.

Philippe Brais and Gérald Fauteux (who will later be appointed a Superior Court judge and then a Supreme Court judge) represent the Department of Justice at the time of Rose's trial. Jean de Grandpré helps them prepare the case. Officers of the Royal Canadian Mounted Police (RCMP) also lend their assistance. De Grandpré will never forget the painstaking work he was given.

> I did the research, the field work. I was trying to disentangle this knot, all the code names used. It was a complex ring, a real maze. But I did it and was able to see everything clearly.

The list of the sixty-three code names identified by de Grandpré is published in the report by the Royal Commission (Taschereau-Kellock) set up in 1946 to determine ways to strengthen security measures in Canada.

In search of lost treasure

Autumn 1939. Hitler readies to invade Poland. The Polish authorities move quickly to protect a national treasure: tapestries, jewels, royal garments, and silverware, most of which date from the fifteenth century. After many twists and turns, the items end up in Canada, in trunks. A Polish diplomat settled in Canada sends the trunks to Ottawa and Sainte-Anne-de-Beaupré, a town in Québec City. Later, the treasures are stored with the Ursulines convent in Québec City, but it is all very hush-hush. The Polish authorities make a diplomatic request for police assistance and declare their intention to take legal action to recover the treasure. They mandate the Brais firm to prepare a legal case that can be submitted to an Ontario or Québec court, a goal that will ultimately not be achieved. Meanwhile, the RCMP locate the trunks containing the treasure in the catacombs of Hôtel-Dieu de Québec. Jean de Grandpré is mandated to take inventory.

> I had to make sure that the treasure was still safe. So I went to the Ursulines. Accompanied by their lawyer, I went into the vaults to make a list of the items. Everything was there. It was impressive.

With the process complete, the federal government is now willing to return the treasure. But staunch anti-Communist Maurice Duplessis is not. The new Polish government displeases the Québec premier, who loudly proclaims that Poland will not be recovering its treasures as long as it is under the boot of a satellite regime of the USSR. It is only when Duplessis dies, and the government of Jean Lesage comes to power in the early 1960s, that an agreement is struck and the treasure is returned to its country of origin. The saga lasts more than twenty years. During that period, even though hundreds of people are involved in the operation, not a single item of the cargo goes missing.

Cases big and small

Daily law practice isn't always like a mystery novel. Far from it. But it has its advantages. Insurance law, the Brais firm's field of expertise, offers de Grandpré an inexhaustible learning environment because it exposes him to a range of legal domains – corporate law, commercial law, civil liability, and litigation – as well as the procedure and day-to-day circumstances of the courts.

Back in the 1940s and 1950s, the insurance industry is much different from what it is today. Disputes in varied forms are the bread and butter of law firms and very often end up in court. At the time, the welfare state is in its infancy, and the public insurance systems we know today would only be set up much later: the Québec auto insurance plan is created in 1978 and, the year after, the Commission de la santé et de la sécurité du travail (later renamed the Commission des normes, de l'équité, de la santé et de la sécurité du travail, or CNESST).

Throughout this period, the insurance sector also wields considerable influence over the economy – a position entrenched by its extraordinary wealth. Large companies often owe their financing to the participation of a major insurance company. It is only in the middle of the post-war boom that the order will change and banks will take over the reins.

In this context, lawyers are important players in society. Renowned jurists are summoned by governments and public bodies to sit on commissions of inquiry, committees, and advisory groups. Others are involved in social organizations, to advise them, take part in their administration, or promote them. Jean de Grandpré takes on commitments of this kind very early in his career. Fernand Graton, one of the great musicians of his generation, founds the Orchestre symphonique des jeunes de Montréal in 1945. He asks de Grandpré to be chair and promote the orchestra to the Montréal public. The young lawyer agrees on the spot.

Luck continues to shine on Jean de Grandpré. Not only is he working in a core sector of society, but he joins a prestigious firm, Brais and Campbell, the same one he worked for during his law studies. At the time, Philippe Brais is one the highest-profile lawyers in Canada and one of the most influential citizens in Montréal. During the 1930s and 1940s, Brais sits on the boards of the most powerful companies in the country (Canadian Pacific Railway, Sun Life Assurance Company of Canada, National Bank of Canada, etc.) and numerous organizations. In 1944 and 1945, he is elected president of the Canadian Bar Association. Brais also makes his entry into politics, both at the federal and provincial level. He is appointed member of the Legislative Council of Québec in 1940 and will later become its president.

Philippe Brais's network of contacts and experience make things that much easier for the young recruit. But Brais is much more than a mentor for de Grandpré. Years later, Brais's daughter would say, "Papa was very proud of him. Jean was his spiritual son in a sense; he had a very strong ethical commitment and took the firm's affairs to heart."

They are a team for six years, and then, having gained experience, de Grandpré starts looking to spread his wings. In 1949, at the age of twenty-seven, with his brother Louis-Philippe and a partner Harold Tansey, he starts his own firm: Tansey, de Grandpré & de Grandpré. The three lawyers tap into their networks and quickly put together a select list of clients. The biggest names in insurance are there: Lloyd's of London, Sun Alliance, Commercial Union, Prudential, Allstate, Chubb, Continental, Royal Assurance, Western Assurance, and more. In no time, the firm becomes a leader in insurance law in Québec and across Canada.

> We decided that my brother Pierre, President of the Bar of Montréal, wouldn't be joining us. We didn't want Tansey to be surrounded by three brothers. And we didn't want to put all our eggs in the same basket. Pierre had a really great career.

Rigour, integrity, humanity

During his years of legal practice, Jean de Grandpré is often at the centre of many disputes. Some of them stand out in his memory and testify to his rigour and his attention to accuracy and detail.

> In the late 1940s, I represented a businessman who planned to build a movie theatre at the corner of Papineau and Ste-Catherine streets. The land he wanted was right beside a service station. The city was refusing to issue the permit because, under a municipal bylaw, it was forbidden to set up a gas station right next to a public place. I pleaded before the municipal administration and the courts that the bylaw did not apply for the following reason: my client was not asking to build a service station next to a public place, but, on the contrary, to build a movie theatre next to a gas station. They decided that I was right, and my client was able to build his establishment.

The Champlain is inaugurated in 1948. It is the first movie theatre to show films in French in Montréal.

Two other cases highlight just how imprecise certain legal and regulatory texts can be – a weakness de Grandpré always exposes.

> In the 1950s, the A&P grocery chain was looking to open a store on a small street next to the Atwater Market. A municipal bylaw stipulated that there could be no grocery store less than 1,500 feet from a public market. I checked and found that the planned establishment would be 2,500 feet away. I asked the municipal employees how they had obtained a result so different from mine. The answer was that they had calculated it on a map, as the crow flies. I simply told them, "I don't know many people in that sector who do their shopping as the crow flies." The grocery was able to open its doors.

There is also the Linen Supply affair. Linen Supply is an American company that plans on opening in Montréal. At the time, the Montréal clothes cleaning market is made up of small shops. They decide to join forces to fight the invasion. Linen Supply reacts immediately, accusing them of forming a monopoly. The government takes cognizance of it and begins a trial. Jean de Grandpré organizes the defence with Guy Favreau. The two lawyers plead that the law on monopolistic practices essentially concerns the sale of goods. Yet Montréal cleaners are not offering goods, but services alone. The judge rejects the defence. The case goes to appeal. Ultimately, the government relents and the laundries get off with a ridiculously low fine.

If de Grandpré tells these stories today, he insists it's not out of conceit.

> I could very well have lost those cases, you know. That's not what's important. What's important is to make clear how necessary it is for a legislator to be specific, to not leave any room for interpretation. And that goes for every era. Past and present.

It is a rigour Jean de Grandpré always imposes on himself. Check, gather material, double check. He leaves no stone unturned.

Right from the beginning at Brais and Campbell, the young lawyer does not go unnoticed. His work ethic and sense of responsibility are recognized. Later, when he joins forces with his brother, the firm takes in interns in training from McGill University. One of them, Francis Fox, will later become federal communications minister and de Grandpré's sparring partner in the courts. Fox will emphasize the intelligence and integrity of both brothers.

De Grandpré recalls an episode that convincingly demonstrates his methodical mind. The event takes place in the 1980s when he is chancellor of McGill, but the anecdote dates back to the time when he was a partner at Tansey, de Grandpré & de Grandpré.

> At a convocation ceremony – this was in the '80s, when I was chancellor of McGill – I recognized the daughter of a friend of mine, who had died in a terrible accident several years before. I was a lawyer at the time and tutored his three daughters. When she came up on stage, I hugged her like I did when she was a little girl, which made the audience laugh – it was a solemn event.

At the time, the lawyer had gone to great lengths to protect his friend's children.

> When the accident occurred, the burning question was whether he had been the driver or the passenger. If he was driving, there was no redress possible. If he was the passenger, the driver was responsible and a claim could be made to his insurance company. My brother and I went straight away to the place of the accident and to the garage where they had towed the car. No one had touched it yet. And we found proof that the father was indeed the passenger: his shoe was under the driver's seat, so he was sitting in the back. I was lucky: the insurer was my client. The claim was considerable, but we settled it easily. I became the family's tutor, and our investigation made it possible for them to have a certain level of material comfort.

The humanity Jean de Grandpré demonstrates in the case would later be put in the service of a range of cases. Over the course of his legal career, it is in seeking justice that he reveals his true self. Like the time when one of his important clients – a major insurance company – asks him to contest a claim that he deems well-founded. If the company contests the claim (whose value exceeds the limit of the insurance policy), the insured party risks having to pay the surplus.

> There was no reason for them not to pay it. But they were asking me to change my opinion for no good reason. It was unacceptable! I handed the company back the entire file. I told myself, "If a firm is willing to do that, it will do it again later on; maybe they'll even hide things from me in accident reports." I didn't hesitate for an instant; I broke my ties with the company.

Jean de Grandpré does not often represent claimants; insurance companies are his main clients. But, one day, as circumstances have it, he defends a motorcyclist. The young man – in his early twenties – is the victim of a serious accident and is permanently disabled.

> I obtained a very large indemnity from the insurance company. I had the young man come to my office. I had the cheque in my hand. I told him: "I'm not giving you this cheque. If I give it to you, in three years' time you'll have nothing left; you'll be mobbed by a crowd of people who will promise you the moon. I suggest instead that you put the money in a trust, which will pay you an annual pension. Take your time, talk to your friends and family and come back and see me.

The young man will ultimately take his advice.

How to win and lose, brilliantly

Labour law is another important part of Jean de Grandpré's career. He often represents employers' organizations in negotiations. He is the legal adviser, for instance, to the Commission des transports de Montréal.

When construction of the Montréal metro is being planned, a dispute arises between the commission and Jean Drapeau, the city's all-powerful mayor. The commission's engineers are convinced that if the city opts for cars with rubber tires it is committing a serious error. Their argument: the tunnels are not constructed to allow enough fresh air to enter and, therefore, reduce the heat produced by the tires. Because the network is planned to extend underground, this would incur additional costs.

There are several other reasons for metal wheels: they are cheaper, they are manufactured in Montréal (the rubber wheels are produced in France), they do not require aeration pipes, etc. This time, the lawyer fails to convince the National Assembly's committee. "I lost, but brilliantly," de Grandpré jokes today. "With the consequences we now know." (The metro could not be outside because the rubber wheels were not compatible with Montréal winters, and chimneys had to be built to provide aeration.)

Naturally the lawyer will not win all of his cases. But there is no denying his success, as one of his colleagues confirms.

> He was the type of lawyer who could have worked in any field, on any problem. He grasped every aspect of a question so easily; he was able to assimilate complex elements and make them simple.[1]

De Grandpré particularly remembers a torrid dispute between two professional bodies, architects and engineers, in the early 1950s. He will handle the complex dossier with his friend Guy Favreau, the very man who will give his name to the main federal government building in Montréal (200 René-Lévesque Boulevard West).

> The two corporations had their knives drawn. Who should be the project manager on a worksite? The problem seemed insoluble. Guy represented the engineers, I, the architects. The situation was so tense that we asked the presidents of the two associations to give us all the latitude necessary to

1 Surtees, *Pa Bell*, 35.

> unravel this Gordian knot. We had to write up a draft bill and submit it to the National Assembly. Ultimately, the law was adopted to the satisfaction of both parties.

Guy Favreau will later be appointed minister of justice and attorney general of Canada (1964–65). He calls on de Grandpré to settle another difficult question: the Mohawks of Caughnawaga (Kahnawake today) are refusing to allow the St Lawrence Seaway to cross over their lands. The case is before the Court of Appeal, and the minister's lawyer is away in Japan. The hearing is supposed to take place in ten days. Any delay will have serious consequences on the work in progress.

> When Favreau contacted me, I told him right away that I knew nothing of treaties and agreements. He put me in contact with his civil servants, and for a few days I got some intensive training. And Guy knew that the government was still refusing to repay me for the gratuities I had covered when I was a lawyer for the Fowler Commission, some time before. A bureaucracy problem. I pleaded, the judgment was rendered – which was favourable to us – and I took the steps to have the land repossessed. At the scheduled time, the RCMP showed up on site with the necessary equipment. It was deserted. The affair was settled. When he received my bill, Guy called me to tell me that the amount was reasonable, that he had the cheque in his hand and that there would be no discussion this time, no delay.

The lawyer has excellent memories of his friend and remains sad to this day at how his career ends. When Favreau resigns as a result of the Rivard Affair[2] in 1965, his health deteriorates rapidly and he dies two years later, at the age of fifty. "Politics killed him," says de Grandpré.

2 In January 1964, Lucien Rivard is accused of drug trafficking by the U.S. Department of Justice. U.S. Attorney General Robert Kennedy demands his extradition to the United States. Some months later, certain members of the Liberal government are suspected of putting pressure on the judicial system to obtain Rivard's release on bail. Guy Favreau, then attorney general of Canada, receives mitigated blame in the affair, and his government, led by Lester B. Pearson, abandons him.

The last case

In 1966, de Grandpré is still practising as a general counsel. In a few months' time, he will join Bell, but he does not know that. De Grandpré is mandated to defend the company before the Québec Minimum Wage Commission. The commission adopts a rule that requires Bell to make an annual contribution, one that has a good chance of being perpetuated indefinitely. The affair goes to the Supreme Court. Jean de Grandpré organizes his defence around one argument: Bell is a federally chartered institution and, as such, cannot be forced to pay a contribution that is imposed by a provincial organization. The court decides that he is right.

> It was my last visit to the Supreme Court. As I left, I hung up my gown for good.

A sought-after man

Over the course of his legal career, Jean de Grandpré is involved in a number of parallel activities that increase his stature and the reputation of his firm. In 1955, he is named legal adviser for the Royal Commission on Broadcasting (Fowler Commission). He plays an active part in writing the final report with his colleague John Coyne, the other legal adviser on the commission. Here again he is noticed for his painstaking work.

> I was meticulous about syntax. So much so that some people found it amusing and kept saying, "There's a French-Canadian here who's telling us how to write English."

The commission also assigns him the task of writing a draft bill on radio broadcasting, which it intends to propose to the government (it is published as an appendix to the report). The newly elected Diefenbaker government is quick to adopt a new law, whose content is largely inspired by the commission's text. Among the most important provisions is the creation of the Canadian Radio-television Commission, precursor of the Canadian Radio-television

Jean de Grandpré will receive another offer from the political establishment, this time in 1971 while working at Bell. It is the time of Québec's great hydroelectric projects, and Premier Robert Bourassa has just launched the latest behemoth, which will harness the rivers of James Bay.

> Robert Bourassa was pressuring me to take over the management of the James Bay Development Corporation (JBDC), which had just been created. I was flattered, but I couldn't accept his offer for two reasons: firstly, I was then the executive vice president in charge of half of Bell's operations and I had the chairmanship in my sights; secondly, I was convinced that the company would be controlled by Hydro-Québec, which would greatly limit the JBDC leaders' margin of manoeuvrability. And that's exactly what happened. Ultimately, time proved me right. And I never regretted my decision.

and Telecommunications Commission (CRTC) – ironically, the same federal regulatory body with which Jean de Grandpré would later cross swords at Bell.[3]

More than once over the course of his career, de Grandpré is called on to fulfill other functions. A political position is offered to him in the early 1950s.

> While Guy Favreau and I were eating lunch on Dufferin Terrace in Québec City, a Liberal Party organizer introduced himself to us. He was looking for candidates for the next election. Favreau said he was thinking about it – we know what happened next. For me, it was a categorical no. I valued my freedom too much.

As a lawyer, Jean de Grandpré is very active on several fronts. In 1961, he is appointed a member of the board of directors of the Barreau du Québec. He also holds a position on the board of directors of

---

3 Surtees. *Pa Bell*, 37.

the École des hautes études commerciales de Montréal (HEC). In 1965, he becomes the first Canadian lawyer to sit on the executive committee of the International Association of Insurance Counsel, a prominent American organization. Those are his final steps as a lawyer. He will soon be making his entrance as a top-tier manager.

Jean de Grandpré greatly appreciated his years of law practice and could very well have continued in law.

> The practice of law is so alive. You meet so many people from different fields. You have to analyze complex questions, decipher things, develop arguments. Sometimes it's difficult to set aside your emotions, but it's absolutely necessary. In short, legal practice is demanding, creative work that is anything but routine.

Did law prepare him for the challenges he will face as a senior corporate executive? He would give this answer in 1973, after his first few years at Bell.

> There's no denying that it's difficult to completely break free from a first discipline. Your first reaction is to consider a problem from that angle, but I'm trying to get away from that attitude. In the company, I try hard to behave as a generalist.[4]

Clearly, it is impossible to confine Jean de Grandpré to just one discipline. In each and every one, however, he is a leader.

4 Bantey, "Un homme pas compliqué," 25.

3

The Bell Years (1966–76)

THE ASCENT

Jean de Grandpré's arrival at Bell marks the starting point of a success story that will span more than two decades – one that will lead the firm and its acclaimed manager to the pantheon of Canadian industry. In 1966, Bell has just completed twenty successful years. Two forces power its spectacular growth: the explosive demand for telecommunications services and the rapid evolution of technology. But no one has seen anything yet. The real technological explosion is just around the corner: Bell will grasp telephony's technological shift before everyone else and stand as a pioneer as a new world of telecommunications opens up.

The outsider

Nothing seemed to predestine Jean de Grandpré to one day lead Bell. In the early 1960s, the lawyer has a brilliant career in law and shows no particular interest in telephone services or the telephone industry in general. The first contact is established in 1964. Without success. The telephone industry at the time was calling for a rate review. A lawyer named John O'Brien, on contract with Bell to prepare hearings for the Canadian Transport Commission – then the body in charge of regulating telephone services – asks de Grandpré to work with him. But O'Brien is cryptic: Bell requires the utmost discretion and he may not reveal the content of the case or even the name of the firm. This is all too vague for de Grandpré and he refuses outright. The relationship between the two colleagues remains unchanged as they are long-standing acquaintances and collaborate occasionally; their firms, moreover, are friendly (they would merge in the late 1970s).

A few weeks later, however, O'Brien repeats the offer. This time with more insistence. O'Brien is recovering from an illness, but,

WHY REGULATE TELEPHONE SERVICES?

Why did governments impose rules on the telephone industry instead of letting the laws of the market do their work as they did in other sectors of the economy? Because, right from the start, the telephone was considered a universal public service: everyone had to have access to one as the network developed. This character of universality also implied that services had to be offered at reasonable rates.

Governments could have chosen to build the new public service infrastructure themselves – in principle. But because they didn't have the necessary expertise, they chose to entrust the construction of the network and the development of the services to private enterprise – while imposing certain rules. Regulations would, however, evolve significantly from the time the first telephones became available at the end of the nineteenth century.

The Bell Telephone Company of Canada is founded in Montréal in 1880. A federal law governs its actions and stipulates its duties and powers. The company receives authorization to erect telephone lines that cross or border public properties and rights of way. That privilege will soon be coupled with obligations.

In 1906, the Board of Railway Commissioners for Canada (the regulatory body at the time) requires that all telephone charges billed to subscribers be first submitted for its approval. The board also acquires the power to oversee the interconnection of Bell's network with the networks of other companies.

In 1967, the government transfers the task of regulating Bell's activities to the Canadian Transport Commission, and then the CRTC takes over the reins in 1976. The main responsibilities of the regulatory bodies are to see that charges are reasonable and fair and that they are not unduly preferential or discriminatory. They also have to approve the terms and conditions for interconnection with other companies. From the late 1960s to as recently as 2000, extended, complicated, and tedious public hearings are held to determine the consequences of diversifying Bell's activities and telecommunications companies in general.

By the end of the 1970s, restrictions on the sector begin to ease, and the loosening continues, timidly at first, throughout the 1980s. But in 1992, there is a dramatic turn of events: the CRTC upends the industry by opening the field of long-distance communications to free competition. This means a stake of $8 billion is being transferred to the free market, nearly half the total revenues of the telecommunications services industry ($17.4 billion in 1993). Similarly, in 1997, the CRTC authorizes competition in the local telephone services and cable distribution markets.

Today, a globalized economy and international trade agreements increasingly limit governments' actions on telecommunications in Canada and around the world. In fact, opening the industry to competition has made detailed regulatory supervision of rates less necessary, so much so that the CRTC no longer intervenes in the retail rates of most communication services. Nowadays, the CRTC serves more to establish the standards and conditions for interconnection between the networks of the former monopolies and the networks of the newcomers to the market. Finally, the CRTC checks that the conditions for competition are properly met and that all players follow the rules of the game.

most crucially of all, the case has taken a new twist. The Canadian Transport Commission plans to modify how subscribers' rates are set. The review is considered necessary because the method in use dates back to 1906. This time, O'Brien answers all of his colleague's questions and immediately invites him to join him in taking on the case. And this time de Grandpré agrees. In the months to come, he will actively work with Bell's lawyers and O'Brien to build an argument. At the time, he has no idea that he is diving into a long and convoluted debate over regulation that would last two decades.

From the very first episode, the affair seems complicated. The Canadian Transport Commission announces a radical change in the regulations: it seeks to re-evaluate the very basis on which Bell's authorized earnings are calculated. The challenge for de Grandpré is not only legal but economic: he has to prepare a strong plea, but also one founded on recognized economic principles. In plain language, it is about devising rules that strike a balance between the interests of telephone service subscribers ("just and reasonable rates," according to the terms of the law) and the interests of the shareholders, since an inflow of capital is essential to Bell's growth.

The logician

Jean de Grandpré accepts the challenge. From the start, he pleads for freedom of enterprise. That will be his credo. De Grandpré argues that Bell does not evolve in a parallel universe, cut off from other commercial activities. He points out that the company not only has to deal with competitors in its sector, but also across the industry in general for labour, materials, management, consumers, and, above all, capital. It must, therefore, be attractive.

But first, to better understand the argument de Grandpré develops with his collaborators, some background is in order. At the time, telephone rates were set according to the "cost-plus method." The rate is established by calculating the service's total production costs (the sum of the inputs: materials, labour, general costs) and adding to it an amount predetermined by the regulatory authority. This added amount is the company's profit.

Jean de Grandpré and his collaborators find the formula counterproductive for a number of reasons. They put forward three arguments to demonstrate as much. First, the formula in no way encourages the search for efficiency in the company and, therefore, compromises its development.

> If, after demonstrating the competence, talent, performance, vision, wisdom, and foresight to improve its services and better respond to needs, the company obtained excellent results but could not profit from this good performance, the management would gradually fall into a routine, and the services' cost price would increase.

Second, the method holds little interest for investors because it considerably limits possibilities for growth. And naturally any company needs capital to grow.

> We sometimes tend to forget that investors are the source of the services offered by Bell. Without their capital, the facilities required would not exist. We can't think of providing the services the public demands without thinking of the interests of the lenders.

Third, de Grandpré argues that the dynamic created by the model will have an impact on subscribers sooner or later.

> If the earnings level cannot match that of the industries with which it competes, its strength will dwindle and the private subscriber will probably be the first affected by such a decline.[1]

These arguments boil down to one and the same conclusion: Bell must be considered and treated like other businesses so it can enjoy the best conditions possible to develop in a competitive market. To reach these objectives, de Grandpré maintains that the current mindset has to be reversed: emphasis on the cost price for services has to go, and profit-seeking take its place. He calls for Bell to adopt a new method, one based on a range of authorized earnings. Under this approach, the company can keep any profit arising from efficiency gains and – as long as this profit remains within an authorized range (e.g., 7 per cent to 10 per cent of earnings) – distribute it to the shareholders. In this case, the de facto emphasis is on the search for efficiency.

The proposal is accepted by the Canadian Transport Commission in May 1965, and Bell can now enjoy a new freedom. As Bell's leaders see it, this latitude should work for everyone: the investors, the business, the employees, and the consumers.

The search for a balance between these groups marks Jean de Grandpré's entire career at Bell Canada, and later at BCE.

1 Surtees, *Pa Bell*, 51.

An offer he couldn't refuse

Simplifying, making things clear, and identifying the issues: those are the strengths of the senior manager Jean de Grandpré will become. The hearings of the Canadian Transport Commission aren't just a forum for de Grandpré's legal prowess; they show the world an executive who can breathe new life into Bell. Marcel Vincent, president at the time, recognized this and invited the lawyer to join Bell as general counsel.[2]

> Marcel Vincent called me and said, "Aren't you tired of climbing that hill? (My office was on Saint-Jacques Street, at the bottom of Beaver Hall Hill.) Come join the team."

Jean de Grandpré knew Bell well. Over the previous two years, he argued back and forth with the company because it had the impertinence to install a defective telephone system in his law firm. And now his adversary was earnestly courting him.

It isn't the first time he is asked to take on the position of general counsel (which he would occupy after the departure of Charlemagne Venne, scheduled for September 1966). A first invitation was extended to him during the Canadian Transport Commission hearings some months before, but he turned it down. The reason given: the fear of being confined to one issue, the fear of routine.

> My first goal was to continue my law practice and not end up in a company. My firm offered me interesting, varied, lively work. But if I could get into a management position, I might consider the offer. I told them what I wanted. The response was negative at first. "We can't guarantee that there'll be any openings in the management team," they told me.

By the time he receives the call from Marcel Vincent, the situation has changed: a certain number of managers have announced their imminent retirement. This time, de Grandpré agrees to meet the head of personnel Jim Hobbs at Vincent's invitation. He is told that they are considering his candidacy for a management position.

2 Marcel Vincent was the first francophone CEO of Bell.

De Grandpré the lawyer takes the plunge. On 1 January 1966 he officially joins the Bell Canada Telephone Company as a member of the legal team. Ever careful, he keeps a window of freedom open.

> They asked me if I wanted a contract, but I didn't want one. I told myself that once I'd start I might not like what they were offering me. Or maybe they themselves wouldn't be satisfied with my work. Time passed. And throughout my whole career at Bell, from 1966 to 1989, I never signed a contract.

Bell's Canadian expansion

In the 1960s, Bell looks to acquire regional telephone companies. The stated objective: to position Bell as the key player in the telephone industry in Canada. The underlying goal: to prevent the U.S. holding company General Telephone & Electronics Corporation (GTE) (which became Bell Atlantic Corporation in 1983 and then Verizon Communications in 2000) from taking control of small regional companies. If that happens, there is a big risk GTE will have a stranglehold on the entire continent's communications routing via the American network. The very future of the TransCanada Telephone System would be compromised.

But the government doesn't trust Bell. Word is going around that the company is becoming a monopoly. It is a complicated situation. And when things get complicated, as they do in the negotiations over the takeover of the Maritime Telegraph and Telephone Company (MT&T), you call in a lawyer. In Nova Scotia, Jean de Grandpré comes up against a fearsome adversary, Robert Stanfield, then provincial premier (a few months later he would become leader of the federal Progressive Conservative Party). The power struggle ends in Ottawa before the regulatory authority: de Grandpré obtains the authorization he needs to issue the shares required for the transaction. Bell then becomes the majority shareholder (52.4 per cent) of MT&T. But, by virtue of a provision adopted by the Nova Scotia Legislature, it would not be able to vote the shares. For Jean de Grandpré, it is expropriation in disguise. He could contest the manoeuvre before the courts, but declines to do so. "Instead, I recommended to the Bell board that it work with the MT&T management. And that proved to be a success."

The experience would be instructive. De Grandpré learns a lesson that he would apply in subsequent transactions.

> Going forward, it seemed more effective to opt for partial control; minority interests would then serve as natural intermediaries in Bell's policies. American Telephone and Telegraph (AT&T) managers in the United States made the mistake of systematically taking 100 per cent control. They, therefore, deprived themselves of getting the necessary support in the business community in which they wanted to set up shop.[3]

The strategy: the birth of Bell Canada

Canadians have long accepted the notion that access to telephone services and, more broadly, the diffusion of communications technology, are the shared responsibility of the state and private enterprise.

In the late 1960s, however, the difference between the two parties' outlooks has never been starker. Each player seeks to retain control over a development that could slip through its fingers at any time. The stakes are high, for society and for the company.

On the one hand, the government is basing the legitimacy of its action on the expectations of a population that wants high-quality, accessible services and low costs. On the other, Bell is arguing that to get there, it has to acquire the means to build a top-notch telecommunications network and ensure the company's growth. And what are these means? Continued growth in productivity, which requires latitude, and the development of new technology, which requires substantial investments every year. What's more, Canada is on the brink of an inflationary period – the inflation rate will fluctuate between 9 per cent and 12 per cent in the 1970s – which only exacerbates the need for an injection of funds. In this context, every year, Bell is obliged to formulate a request to increase the rates and submit it to the regulatory authority.

3 Rens, *The Invisible Empire*, 38.

For now, it is open conflict. The government is wary of possible abuse and works to limit Bell's appetite. Whereas at Bell, they deplore the fact that, in some respects, Canadian telecommunications is a success in spite of, rather than because of, government action.

The tension can also be blamed mainly on the fact that the sector is booming: telecommunications is at a watershed moment. The information society is just getting off the ground and the future looks bright. There is no better illustration of this than the example of Northern Electric (which becomes Northern Telecom in 1976 and then Nortel after 1995).

Bell's equipment manufacturer is experiencing tremendous growth. Up until now, Northern Electric has been dependent on products mainly designed and manufactured in the United States. But the context is changing and Bell's leaders have decided that Northern should make a move into international markets. The development raises a fundamental question, one that is the subject of extended debates and multiple public hearings for at least two decades: To what degree should the organization and activities of Bell, including its subsidiaries, be subject to regulatory authority and to what degree should they be left to the laws of the market? The answer to this question will be decisive for the future of Bell, Northern, and the entire Canadian telephone industry. It is in this context that the second round of the duel between Bell and the regulatory authority takes place. Here, once again, Jean de Grandpré will play a decisive role.

Bell's top management believes it is time to modify the company's act of incorporation to adapt it to the industry's situation and current needs. It is a significant challenge. The general counsel has to produce a coherent set of modifications, the most extensive ever proposed by Bell. To prepare the groundwork – and knowing that the opposition will be fierce – de Grandpré rents a hotel room in Ottawa. He will spend most of his time there for some fifteen months. Hélène, his wife, moves in with him. He takes advantage of his time there to cultivate relations with elected officials and high-level bureaucrats. But above all, he works actively with the government's lawyers to fine-tune the private bill that will become the company's new charter.

The amendments promise big changes. Jean de Grandpré proposes to update the definition of Bell's activity, replacing "telephone" with "telecommunications"; to clarify and regularize the links between Bell and Northern Electric; to authorize both companies to invest in R&D; to issue shares without the approval of the regulatory body; and, finally, to change the name of the company, which will henceforth be called Bell Canada.

The changes raise concerns, even at Bell. The original names, in English and French, have to be kept (because of the shares in circulation). But to add another one? Paul Lesage, brother of Jean Lesage – the former premier recognized as the father of the Quiet Revolution in Québec – is in charge of registering trade names in the federal government. He rules that the addition is impossible. Jean de Grandpré brings out the big guns: "Your brother used the same process for Hydro-Québec in 1962. So why can't Bell do it too?" Lesage magnanimously agrees.

But Bell's intentions still raise objections of another kind this time. A group of members of Parliament (MPs) are intent on blocking it at every turn. The bill dies on the order paper the first time, in the fall 1967 session. The work has to be started from scratch in the next session (and another $750,000 in fees paid to file the power of attorney and the motion); de Grandpré has to marshal solid arguments on crucial points. Just replacing the word telephone with telecommunications raises the ire of radio broadcasters, television broadcasters, and cable television operators and dismays the nascent information processing industry. All fear that Bell is using the provision as a pretext to infiltrate their domains. De Grandpré works very hard to reassure the committee, the government's representatives, and the interest groups.

> Our goal was to make Bell a telecommunications company and not just a telephone company. We had no intention of becoming a radio or television broadcaster, cable television operator, or publisher that would shape the country's thinking. We just wanted to have the possibility of relaying the signals emitted by the radio and television broadcasters.

This assurance satisfies the legislators, but not the radio and television broadcasters. So Bell agrees to add two clauses to the bill to make things very clear.

The MPs are much less conciliatory when it comes to Bell's motion to issue shares without the approval of the regulatory authority. Numerous interest groups unconditionally support them. In the face of such opposition, de Grandpré reacts with diplomacy: "If that makes you uncomfortable, even if we think that it remains a pointless regulation, we are entirely prepared to remove this clause in the bill and allow the Canadian Transport Commission the authority to control the issue of shares."[4]

But de Grandpré is not a quitter. It was only a matter of time before he would apply the measure again, a full sixteen years later. But, for now, something else catches his attention because it, too, is arousing suspicion: the links between Bell and its equipment manufacturer Northern Electric. Jean de Grandpré explains:

> It was not clear at the time that Bell had the right to hold a manufacturing company. For us, it was essential! The future of the two companies, the growth prospects the market was offering, development on an international scale – all of this indicated that we had to build ties and that those ties had to be recognized and accepted.

And what were they so afraid of exactly?

> That Bell was paying too much for the equipment produced by Northern and that it was passing on the bill to subscribers (by increasing rates). In short, they were afraid of establishing a cartel.

De Grandpré thinks he has a good argument to challenge the MPs' opposition. In his view, the manoeuvre poses no risk and it isn't necessary to go through a tender process to dispel doubts. Northern Electric has a number of clients, both in Canada and,

4 Surtees, *Pa Bell*, 120.

increasingly, in the United States – competitors of Bell that buy the same products. And if ever the firm is buying at a higher price than the others, de Grandpré maintains it will be held to account for it the next day. The argument seems foolproof, but it is received with caution.

To assuage the MPs' fears, de Grandpré asks to meet with the caucus of each of the three political parties represented in Parliament. The Liberals and the Progressive Conservatives agree. The meetings take place and the elected representatives are receptive to the requests to amend the company's act of incorporation. Except on one point: Bell's control over Northern Electric. The New Democratic Party (NDP) refuses to take part in the exercise at all. "It's never been done," argues leader David Lewis. But Lewis puts de Grandpré in contact with his communications critic Ed Schreyer (who would later become governor general of Canada), and the Manitoban MP ends up becoming a valuable ally. Jean de Grandpré obtains Schreyer's assent, and, in his turn, Schreyer convinces his new leader Ed Broadbent – David Lewis has just departed – of the merit of Bell's request. There is a dramatic about-face: the NDP gives its support, and the new charter is adopted. It is a complete surprise because de Grandpré has always belonged to the big Liberal family. He never would have believed that a party from the left, with few affinities with businesspeople, would save the day.

On that day "The Bell Telephone Company of Canada" officially becomes "Bell Canada." It is March 1968. The company is now in an excellent position to move forward into the information society.

The reformer

Innovation often comes from outside. It doesn't take long for Jean de Grandpré to breathe new life into the organization. Only a few months after his arrival, he receives a promotion: the general counsel becomes vice president. And one of his first decisions on taking the position is to decentralize. The vice presidency of the legal department will now be divided into three sections: General Administration, East (Québec), and West (Ontario) (the vast majority of Bell's services are concentrated in the two provinces).

The operation is hailed by the senior management as a success. The reason for his decision is still very clear to him five decades later.

> The thing that hit me as soon as I stepped into the position was that Bell formed a monolithic block; the structure was rigid, hierarchical; all the decisions were made by a few individuals at the top. For me, that was certainly a source of inefficiency.

By the end of the 1960s, Bell already has a long history. As it evolved, the company developed a managerial culture based on experience and internal promotion. You make your career at Bell, you get trained there, and you climb the ladder, rung by rung.

But Jean de Grandpré does not come from the company's old boys' club, like most of his colleagues. He isn't well-versed in Bell's culture. Later on, he will be the first CEO to come from outside the company – his predecessor, Marcel Vincent, joined Bell back in 1927. This independence of mind, combined with his skills as a manager, gives him an advantage that works in his favour more than once. Modestly, Jean de Grandpré attributes his success to plain old luck: "I was simply the right man at the right place at the right time."

Jean de Grandpré is nothing if not a lucky guy. Only a few months after his appointment to the vice presidency of the legal department, the seat of vice president of administration opens up. De Grandpré's ambitions are known. He is offered the key position in the company, and he accepts without hesitation. That was in 1968, less than two years after he joined the company. De Grandpré now has a front-row seat. His career as a lawyer, to which he has devoted nearly three decades, ends here. But the litigant skills he has developed over the years will serve him for a long time.

Observers also note how accurate his knowledge of economics is.

> "There were few men who had as keen an interest or a detailed understanding of economic issues," said Bruce Scott, professor at Harvard Business School. "He had a very complete understanding of economic issues and public policies."[5]

5 Surtees, *Pa Bell*, 54.

MANAGEMENT: RETURNING TO HIS BASE

"My employees didn't work for me; they worked with me." For Jean de Grandpré, any manager worth their salt must never forget their base. It is impossible to make a success of a large business otherwise. And it is a principle he will wisely put into practice. An example:

> The cafeteria at Bell always stayed open overnight to accommodate the telephone operators on duty. But at a certain point, I was getting wind that one of my managers was thinking of closing it at night, on the pretext that doing so would save some $50 thousand. That made no sense to me! But the idea was already circulating among the staff. I went to meet with the overnight operators at work. I wanted to reassure them, to tell them that, on that night, and on all the other nights to come, they could have hot soup, have an omelet cooked for them, or simply relax in a friendly place and drink their coffee. In short, that there was no question, even for one minute, that they would be deprived of a service essential to their well-being. The cafeteria stayed open.

Neither will the CEO hesitate to go out into the field to ask his linemen what they think of a potential change in their working hours.

> These employees were working forty hours per week, spread out over five days. But when they left the work centre, they often had to drive twenty-five to thirty kilometres before arriving at the place where they had to do the job. This travelling time was counterproductive. To get around the problem, some managers were proposing the following solution: if [the crew] worked ten hours a day concentrated over four days, they would spend less time on the road and could stay longer on site when needed, instead of returning the next day. We would be saving time and money. But I was getting conflicting opinions on whether this was a good idea. I didn't conclude either way, but decided to go to meet the parties in question and get their opinions. And so

> it was one morning, very early, I found myself in Black Lake, Ontario, in a work centre in front of a group of linemen who were getting ready to fill their orders for the day. I told them about the plan. I got three types of reactions. The young single guys were in favour of the ten-hours-over-four-days formula; the idea of having three days off to go hunting, fishing, or partying suited them just fine! The married men and the dads were much less open to the idea; they thought their wives would detest the formula because it would require them to handle the nightly routine with the kids alone. They told me, "If you do that, things will go very badly at home." The last group, the married men without children, leaned the same way, reckoning that having one more day off would just be a chance to spend more on trips, eating out, and other pastimes. "We can't afford it," they told me. I was set. We kept the schedule as it was.

Jean de Grandpré confirms that he has always been interested in such issues. But he believes that what is Caesar's should be rendered unto Caesar.

> When I arrived at Bell, I was put in contact with the vice president of finance, George Wallace. It was he who initiated me into the mysteries of high finance. I knew relatively little in that area (a little accounting – assets, liabilities, depreciation, amortization, reserve funds, etc.), but negotiating loans for tens and even hundreds of millions was outside my scope of knowledge. Wallace took me under his wing. He was a skilled and charming man. I spent two years with him, which allowed me to better grasp the financial and administrative challenges Bell was facing.

At the same time, de Grandpré builds strong relationships in the financial world. On the company board, where he sits as vice president, he meets Herbert Lank, then president of the multinational DuPont in Canada and a director at the Toronto-Dominion (TD) Bank. Lank asks him to become a director of DuPont Canada. "There was never a doubt that Lank was my mentor in the financial world," Jean de Grandpré acknowledges gratefully. Lank puts him in contact with Allen Lambert, then CEO of TD Bank. Lambert asks him to become a director of TD. Lank also introduces him to other people who would open doors to boards of directors and other centres of decision-making.

As soon as he joins the administration, the new vice president begins replicating the model he has established in the legal department. This time, he decentralizes everything by creating Québec and Ontario regions as centres for decision-making and operations. For Québec francophones, the gesture is much more than an administrative one. It allows them to work in French in Québec and climb the company ladder in their own language. It is a first in Bell's history.

That is how de Grandpré, who spent his entire career as a lawyer in English and who always refused to be labelled a French-Canadian, did more for the advancement of French in his home province than the leaders who preceded him. The operation is hailed by senior management, who are sensitive to Québecers' growing desire for self-affirmation. It is the Quiet Revolution: Québec is booming and asserting its determination to live in French and to use its economic leverage like never before.

At Bell, Jean de Grandpré's career is off to a flying start. After his time in administration, he is offered another promotion: in 1970, he becomes vice president of the Eastern Region. De Grandpré will now familiarize himself with operations.

> The Eastern Region encompassed half of Bell's subscribers. It was all of Québec and two thirds of Ontario – the territory that extended from northern Toronto to the Manitoba border. I had to travel a lot.

Once again, luck smiled: de Grandpré finds an exceptional ally in the organization, Robert Carlton Scrivener. Both men share the same vision. It is they who will be the great architects of Bell's and Northern's rapid development over the next fifteen years.

4

The Bell Years (1976–83)
THE SUMMIT

In 1976, Jean de Grandpré becomes chairman and CEO of Bell Canada, the most prominent position in the country. The new CEO has big ambitions for his company. Three objectives underpin his actions: innovate, diversify, and internationalize. The signing of a lucrative contract in Saudi Arabia thrusts Bell onto the international stage. The holding company plans to gradually expand its presence around the world. Yet the Canadian regulatory straitjacket keeps reining it in. The battle will be fierce.

From the start, the fates of Jean de Grandpré and Robert Scrivener seem sealed. Scrivener becomes president in 1968, just when de Grandpré takes on the position of vice president of administration. Scrivener is named chair and CEO in 1973; de Grandpré is promoted to president. And when Scrivener leaves Bell for Northern in 1976, de Grandpré succeeds him. There is no question of favouritism here. Nor is it a matter of political calculation by Bell's management (de Grandpré is a francophone, and Bill 101 is making headlines at this time). As a telecommunications expert notes, "No one at the time thought for a moment to attribute his appointment to the fact that he was a francophone; de Grandpré was simply the best manager of his generation."[1]

It's worth mentioning here that, in the 1970s, managing Bell is considered the most important position in the private sector in Canada.

Scrivener and de Grandpré are visionaries. Both see the direction telecommunications is taking and envision big things ahead for the Bell group in a changing world. While the first prepares to take over the reins of Northern, the future Bell CEO rapidly assimilates

1 Rens, *Invisible Empire*, 40.

the challenges he is about to take on in a time of economic and technological turbulence. He develops the tools that will make him one of the finest strategists and most skilled tacticians of his era.

As for Scrivener, he grasps before anyone else in the industry the central role information technology will soon play in communications. He urges Bell to go digital, a gamble that pays enormous dividends. In 1976, he makes a surprising choice and leaves the top management of Bell for the position of president of Northern. From this rostrum, he will drive the Bell subsidiary's spectacular growth and makes it a world player.

At a basic level, de Grandpré and Scrivener believe it is essential to capitalize on the synergy between the equipment manufacturer (Northern) and the telephone services network (Bell) and make that synergy a driver of growth. The other subsidiaries and associated companies also have to be included when the right project or contract comes along. And the Canadian territory offers a unique field of experimentation, so numerous are its challenges: the low population density, the climate, the huge expanse.

The strong ties that exist between the Bell group's organizations will yield undreamed-of results. Jean de Grandpré acknowledges as much in the late 1980s, with legitimate pride.

> The combined efforts of the operating, research and development, and manufacturing organizations have advanced this country to the forefront of world telecommunications technology. It is in large measure the close interworking of these vertically integrated members of the Bell Canada family which has led to the company's success.[2]

He sustains this momentum throughout his career at Bell, and even accelerates it when the opportunity arises. Three recurring themes guide his actions: innovate, diversify, and internationalize.

2 Surtees, *Pa Bell*, 218.

Innovate: the ace in the hole

Bell's new charter opens a window of opportunity that will decide its future. Bell Canada obtains permission to join forces with its subsidiary, Northern Electric, to occupy a new niche in Canadian telecommunications: R&D. Bell-Northern Research (BNR) is born in 1969. At the time, the BNR laboratories form the largest independent R&D body in Canada.

Northern is the first to profit from the investments in the labs. It develops equipment that gives it a head start over the rest of the world and positions it among the leaders of the industry. Bell will not be left behind. It is the first company in the world to set up a commercial digital communications network and the first to install a commercial packet-switched communications network (Datapac). Its expertise makes it one of the most innovative firms in the industry. The synergy between Bell and Northern is also a significant asset because it means that innovations can be tested in the field before they reach external markets.

Diversify: the first steps

In any organization, the obvious is often overlooked. For decades at Bell, the publishing of millions of telephone directories was subcontracted out, without a thought to the profit such activity might yield. When de Grandpré and Scrivener agree to diversify the company's operations in the late 1960s, they are quickly faced with a choice.

> One of the first things we looked at was the contract given to an external firm to print the Yellow Pages. We were spending a huge amount of money for work that we could very well do ourselves! We had to find a way to bring this lucrative activity home. But there was a problem.

Bell Canada's charter prohibits investment in a company belonging to another sector outside of telecommunications. Scrivener and de Grandpré were going to find a way to get around the obstacle. The solution comes to them quite naturally: form a new company and tie it to a company controlled by Bell (and which is not subject to the charter). That is how Tele-Direct comes into being in 1971 as a subsidiary of Capital Telephone, a minuscule Ontario firm that operates a few dozen lines in a small village in central Ontario.[3] And that is how the diversification of operations begins.

But the affair threatens to work to Bell's detriment before the regulatory authority.

> In the year Tele-Direct was created, the profits of the company we had been giving the contract to (Ronalds-Federated Limited) were transferred to the new company as profits of the new Bell subsidiary. The amount was, therefore, taken into account in determining the rates. This way of considering Tele-Direct as a component of telephone services was then perpetuated.

Starting the following year, the regulatory authority stipulates that Tele-Direct's profits will be included in the Bell revenues used to set telephone subscribers' rates; according to the body, the directory is a part of telephone services.

Internationalize: the Bell–Northern Electric partnership

The Bell group makes its first real steps on the international stage in Turkey in the late 1960s. Northern Electric obtains a contract from the country's post, telephone and telegraph company for equipment. The contract is considerable in scope and projected to last five years. Northern Electric feels it is in its best interest to form a joint venture with the Turkish company (Northern Electric Telekomünikasyon A.S., or NETA). Northern Electric soon realizes there is going to be more to the contract than producing and selling equipment. It has to train Turkish personnel to install and operate that equipment. This need leads Northern Electric to call on its parent company to set up an international group of consultants, and Bell creates the unit in 1967. The model is born: Northern Electric and Bell will now be working together in external markets. The

3 Rens, *Invisible Empire*, 42.

experience will be repeated in Greece, then Spain, the Philippines, and Nigeria so well that after two years of activity, forty-five Bell employees are acting as consultants in a dozen countries.[4]

A new player: Bell Canada International

As Jean de Grandpré becomes CEO in 1976, he inherits a growing company that dominates the Canadian telecommunications industry. The Bell galaxy has grown considerably, but that isn't enough for him. He has a bigger dream: to make the Bell group a major international company capable of competing with industry leaders all over the world.

> For me, it was essential that Bell went beyond Canadian borders, and that it competed with the biggest players. And growth, necessarily, was achieved by conquering foreign markets. I absolutely failed to understand how anyone could even think otherwise.

The new CEO is a "man of the world." It's in his nature. Faced at a very young age with the two great cultures of Canada, he learns to thrive in diversity and feel at ease in it. One of his first actions is to bring together the consultation services the company offers around the world. A new subsidiary is born: Bell Canada International (BCI). With this unit, de Grandpré has a dual objective: to accelerate Bell's internationalization and shield its activities abroad from the Canadian regulatory straitjacket.

The expedition to Saudi Arabia

A few months after joining Bell's command post, de Grandpré is presented with a rare opportunity. Saudi Arabia plans to modernize and develop its telecommunications network. It launches an international call for tenders, the largest ever issued in the field at the time. Jean de Grandpré recounts how Bell obtained the largest contract in its history abroad.

4 Surtees, *Pa Bell*, p. 220.

It was 1975. The king of Saudi Arabia was looking for a single manager for the entire project. It was impossible for us to take advantage of the Bell-Northern partnership because our equipment manufacturer was not producing equipment capable of resisting infiltration by sand. Robert Scrivener and I identified ITT (International Telephone and Telegraph) as a potential partner. We went to New York to meet with Harold Geneen, who was then president of the American multinational, to gauge his interest. The first meeting was easy. The second, however, took another turn. I was alone; Scrivener had become president of Northern. Geneen made me an autocrat's proposal: he didn't want Bell as a partner, but as a subcontractor. I flatly refused. For me, there was no question of our employees being lorded over by ITT's management and personnel in the field.

Some time later, in 1976, the agent of the king – who had no doubt got wind of the criticism and international dealings around the project – changed the call for tenders. Saudi Arabia was now asking for three contracts: a first for large switches, another for smaller switches, and a third for running the new company.

That same year, 1976, Ericsson was celebrating its centenary. The Canadian lawyer of the Swedish multinational, John Kirkpatrick, a former comrade from McGill, invited me to Stockholm for the celebrations. I took the opportunity to meet with the company's senior management. And we clicked. I pitched my offer of a partnership. The response was positive. The people at Ericsson informed me that they could deliver the large switches and that they already had an agreement with the Dutch company Philips for the smaller ones. The trio was formed and we were all set to go. There was only one detail left to be finalized: Saudi Arabia wanted a fixed price for each contract. Ericsson and Philips didn't see any problem in this; they knew their costs. For us, it was impossible because of unforeseen events. Ericsson and Philips were afraid of losing the contract because of my fears and intransigence. And then the solution came. Yes, we would have a firm price, but the contract would be written in such

> a way that Bell would not be vulnerable to a possible loss. It involved identifying the personnel required to perform the obligations of the contract, and each employee would be paid at a fixed rate, determined ahead of time. On December 14, 1977, the deed was done and the contract was awarded to the three partners. But there was still one important detail to be worked out: the Saudi Arabian authorities insisted that the contract be written in Arabic. To ensure that the text properly reflected the commitment we had made, I asked for a double translation: from Arabic to English and then from English to Arabic.
>
> The outcome confirmed what the prime minister of Lebanon had confided to me a few months before: despite all the visits from the prime minister of the United Kingdom, the president of the United States, and the chancellor of Germany, the king wanted to let them know that their arms sales to Iran were worrying his country. That element certainly played a part.

From 1977 to 1982, during the first five years of the contract (which is also followed by a second five-year phase), Jean de Grandpré leads his troops with an expert hand, meticulously organizing his employees' overseas stays and using diplomacy to settle any differences. The boss leaves nothing to chance.

> The employees in the field had to work with personnel from different cultures – Saudi, Korean, and Tunisian. It was because of their professionalism, their tact, and their broadmindedness that everything went smoothly. Hats off to them. They were model ambassadors for Canada.

Naturally, from the time the contract is signed, the employees are prepared for the job to facilitate integration and limit employee turnover, which is always costly for a project overseas. Jean de Grandpré explains his disarmingly pragmatic strategy.

> Throughout my career, I've always consulted people. In the case of Saudi Arabia, the advice of industrial psychologists

> served as my guide. I understood that I had to proceed in four stages to organize human resources: first, identify the workers you need; then, ask them why they want to travel – to see the country or to work; third, ask if the husband or wife wants to be part of the adventure; and finally, if the candidate has children, remember that integration will be easier if they're younger. In Saudi Arabia, we took these precautions, and employee turnover was never a problem.

Every year, 300 to 520 Bell employees live in Saudi Arabia; during the most active period, there is more than 1,000. The adventure is a success for both parties: Saudi Arabia ascends to the ranks of the countries best served by telecommunications in the world. It has the only network whose every component is leading edge. The others, installed long ago, have to blend the old with the modern, with all the difficulties that entails.

For Bell, the success is complete. The company earns nearly $3 billion from the experience and builds a solid international reputation.

The odyssey in Saudi Arabia gives the company wings. Bell is in the big leagues on the world stage. In 1982, by the end of the first phase of the contract, BCI is simultaneously heading fifty-five projects in twenty-eight countries on five continents. The world telecommunications market is booming, and Bell's employees are criss-crossing the globe, offering their expertise in France, the Netherlands, India, Iraq, the United States, Latin America, and Australia. Northern Telecom and BCI work in synergy for the most part, the way the Scrivener – de Grandpré partnership did: Northern Telecom sells and installs the equipment, while BCI provides the consultancy services needed to run the new networks. The projects are diversified, with everything from collaboration, to publishing directories, setting up terrestrial networks, and installing digital switches in hospitals.[5]

The Saudi adventure is a turning point in the company's history. It considerably changes the way in which the company's managers and employees look at the world and the role they can play in it.

5 Mussio, *Becoming Bell*, 99.

Jean de Grandpré had long been convinced that Bell had a place on the international stage.

> If you're a small architect, you'll only ever be able to construct small buildings.

Jean de Grandpré is no small architect. He has acquired the leverage to not only construct a building, but a whole district of enterprises united under one great banner.

Regulatory turpitude

For all the successes that marked Jean de Grandpré's entrance into Bell in the late 1960s, the hostilities between the regulatory authority and the company aren't coming to an end any time soon. Far from it. Other confrontations follow over the years, one after the other, like a never-ending story. In fact, throughout his entire career at Bell, Jean de Grandpré finds himself at the heart of a permanent conflict pitting his company against the regulatory authority. The lawyer-manager quickly learns the rules of the game. In a period marked by numerous public hearings – arenas of debate over rate increases and the choice of framework imposed on a public services company – de Grandpré shines.

The dazzling development of telecommunications in the 1970s and of the Bell group in particular – which is a major player in the industry – goes a long way toward explaining the conflict. Telephone services are still expanding at a fast clip. Rapid urbanization and the explosion of the suburbs are building pressure to accelerate development on the network. The operation requires significant funds. The challenge is all the greater because Canada – like the entire Western world – has entered an era of high inflation. Jean de Grandpré remembers it well:

> The inflation rate hit historic highs in Canada in the 1970s, fluctuating between 5.6 per cent and 12.6 per cent each year. Inflation is a terrible thing for a regulated company like Bell. You have to find the funds and the possible avenues (increasing your rates, issuing shares, etc.) – the things that

A PERILOUS PARTNER

"When you do business abroad, you have to beware of those ostensibly tempting offers people dangle in front of you."

Jean de Grandpré speaks from experience. In the mid-1980s, during one of his stays in Saudi Arabia, he made the acquaintance of a certain Adnan Khashoggi. The Saudi was one of the richest men in the world – his fortune was estimated at $4 billion – and he had an influential network of relationships in the United States, Europe, and the Middle East. Khashoggi was a mediator in a range of businesses, particularly arms sales. In the financial community, he was nicknamed AK (no doubt in reference to the Soviet assault rifle). But he wasn't talking about weapons when he approached the Bell CEO.

> He simply asked me, like that, "Would you be interested in improving the communications system in Cairo?" I studied the project – carefully. It meant tearing up roads, lots of roads, in an overpopulated city, making traffic impossible. The population would be furious with us. I refused.

Khashoggi made a second attempt, in Toronto this time. Sudan was in his sights. He proposed that de Grandpré set up a communications network in the country, which would allow him to mine the ore-rich subsoil beneath.

My wife was with me at the meeting. She told me firmly, "If you do business with AK, I'm divorcing you." I didn't have any intention to, anyway. So I complied.

Khashoggi was a dandy who surrounded himself with pretty women; de Grandpré had noticed as much. And when he saw him again in New York, he was on his guard.

> I was invited to a reception that he had organized. As soon as I entered the room, I realized that there were very few men, many women, and – I was sure of it – at least one photographer.

For the Bell big boss, it was a detail that set the alarm bells ringing. He learned a lesson from the incident that he would share with his teams in the field in Saudi Arabia, on the day the men were invited on a Mediterranean cruise.

I told them, "Go, but don't go alone; take your wives! It's more prudent." Above all, I didn't want to have to manage compromising photos afterwards.

Some time later, de Grandpré learned that Khashoggi had served as an intermediary for arms sales to Iran, an event that sparked the Iran-gate scandal.

any company has access to – and then you're told you're not allowed to have them.

The regulatory authority is not entirely insensitive to Bell's demands. But more often than not it meets Bell's requests for rate increases with a muddling compromise, which forces the company to jump through administrative hoops, revise its operational planning, and put off planned expansions to its telephone network. Jean de Grandpré is not a man to accept the ritual back-and-forth without a fight, knowing that his cause is just. He can play hardball when he needs to. An illustration:

> I needed $60 million to keep Bell's [AA] listing on the New York Stock Exchange. If the company was discounted, many institutions could no longer buy our bonds [a discount meant there would be an increase in the level of risk]. I asked the Canadian Radio-television and Telecommunications Commission [CRTC] for a rate hike to cover the amount. And what was the CRTC's decision? They gave me $30 million – half! I waited forty-eight hours and then I made an appointment with the president, Ann Carver. I had made my request under oath in a public hearing that lasted ten days. I first declared to her that in my entire life I had never committed perjury: that sixty million was essential for me; all the arguments I had ever made were very real. And I was very clear. I told her, "I will stop construction of the network if I

> do not obtain the amount I am asking you for and for which I hold you responsible." At the time, Toronto was developing at lightning speed, and the network had to follow suit. The Toronto newspapers got into the act. They wrote that I was blackmailing, bullying, etc.

Bill Davis is the premier of Ontario. The province objects to the rate increase Bell is asking for, as do Québec and the municipalities. Davis calls de Grandpré to express his disagreement.

> "You can't do that," he tells me. "I'm about to call an election, and my voters want services." I tell him, "It's your fault; you're refusing our request. If I made an exception for you, what will the others say when I have to say no to them?" If you make a threat and don't follow up on it, you lose all credibility. So I kept my word. And a few months later, the president of the CRTC added the missing $30 million.

Ever the diplomat, he is careful to point out that he saw Bill Davis again.

> Much later, we sat together on the Seagram board of directors in Montréal. And we became good friends.

The impasse

The CRTC replaces the Canadian Transport Commission as the regulatory authority in 1976. The new body arrives on the scene just as the economic context is changing. The West will soon be entering the Reagan-Thatcher era, and the winds of liberalism are blowing strongly. The CRTC has to open up to the free market, just as the Americans did when they completely liberalized the sector years before. But Canada is not exactly a mirror of the United States. And the public hearings over regulations are still going on. Indeed, they become longer and more complex and are eating up huge amounts of cash: at least $15 million per year at Bell, according to one executive at the time.

On the one hand, the CRTC is making decisions that encourage competition. In 1977, for instance, it forces Bell Canada to allow cable distributors to use its posts and cables and, in 1979, stipulates that private lines can be interconnected to the public telecommunications networks. What does that mean? From that time on, subscribers to competitors' computer and telephone communications services can go through the Bell local network. Then, in 1980, the CRTC frees up the market for the sale of telephones and other consumer equipment. Three years later, subscribers are given free rein to buy their own devices from any supplier and plug them in like electrical devices. Previously, they had to rent them from their telephone company, and Bell lost many of its sources of revenue. And on the other hand, a series of decisions are tightening the regulatory straitjacket. To better understand the logic behind the CRTC's prescriptions, you have to look at the goal it is pursuing: to combine the regulated sector with the competitive sector. Bell simply wants to draw a line around what has to be regulated – telephone services – and leave everything else to the laws of the market. It isn't the CRTC's goal that is the problem – Bell's is the same – but the sorting out of what goes where.

At Bell, they can't understand the CRTC's vacillation. It is as if Canada can't reconcile the public interest with supporting its major companies in their efforts to conquer foreign markets. This attitude is anathema to Jean de Grandpré the internationalist. He explains the ambivalence of the rulers of the time as follows:

> Canada has suffered from minority syndrome for a long time – a francophone minority within the country and a Canadian minority within the continent. That's why every time Bell was attacked, we could hear them yelling, "You're too big, you're too powerful!" Nobody ever said we offered bad service, were incompetent, had bad technology. The only accusation they ever made against us was about our size. But … you can't do telephony when you're small.

Today, de Grandpré has not changed his opinion. But he adds a nuance to it.

> I never called into question the legitimacy of the state in regulating public services. Governments are there to protect the collective interest; that's their role. But I always contested abusive regulation because it applied to all of Bell's activities. The company had developed so much over the years and was doing business all over the world. Putting all that in the same package and bundling it up into a rigid framework was counterproductive and unfair!

The feeling that Bell is being treated unfairly is never more keenly felt than in the early 1980s. The CRTC makes a decision that is received like a shockwave at Bell. The regulatory authority is requiring that the company include the revenues of BCI – including those generated by the lucrative Saudi contract – in the calculations for Canadian subscribers' rates. The CRTC is basing its decision on the following argument: Bell has created the subsidiary, financed it, and provided it with most of the human resources needed to start it up. The contracts are being performed by Bell employees on loan to BCI. BCI's revenues, therefore, have to be included in the calculation and, ultimately, be reflected in rate reductions because, according to the CRTC, the expertise of Bell's employees has been acquired with subscribers' money. Jean de Grandpré is still astonished by the decision.

> Every time a subsidiary made profits abroad, the CRTC considered them as Bell's revenues. It made no sense. I asserted that if, one day, we suffered losses, they would have to be applied to the rates as well. The argument was judged inadmissible, which I still don't understand. Their response was, "If there's a loss, don't ask subscribers to subsidize it; that's the shareholders' job." That meant that the shareholders would be assuming all the risks, while the subscribers would be sharing the profits. In financial terms, it made no sense. How do you want to attract investors and build the company's growth with reasoning like that?

Some time later, the CRTC reconsiders the question and dials down the tone. It admits that BCI's revenues are, indeed, distinct from those of the parent company; therefore, they will not be subject to the regulatory framework. But not entirely, because the body is requiring in exchange that BCI pay a royalty to Bell for each employee Bell loans to it – a royalty equivalent to one quarter of their salary. Jean de Grandpré firmly objects.

> If you send an executive overseas and they acquire new skills, you make them a better manager who, upon their return, will earn Bell and its subscribers more. Why should BCI have to pay a premium to Bell on top of that?

He hits a brick wall. BCI is now stuck with a huge burden: the subsidiary has to compete on the market with costs that are 25 per cent higher than those of its competitors. An analyst at the time remarks that telecommunications operators around the world happily joined in these attempts to stifle the Bell group's export capacity; for foreigners, it is one less competitor.[6]

Jean de Grandpré confirms it.

> The problem was not the competition, but the combination of regulation and competition, which created rules that were unequal with those of other international players. We didn't just have to deal with our competitors and interest groups; we had to deal with our government as well.

The year 1981 marks a breaking point. Bell asks for an increase in the general rate and outlines what it thinks should be excluded from regulation. The company maintains, in particular, that the majority of Tele-Direct's activities no longer have anything to do with telephone services.

> Tele-Direct had had its share of successes, like the purchase of British American Bank Note [printing of banknotes,

6 Rens, *Invisible Empire*, 45.

> certificates, etc.] and the acquisition of Case-Hoyt, the American company that colour-printed *Architectural Digest*, the reference in printing. With standards as high as these, we built a great reputation very quickly, and the company prospered.

Tele-Direct expands significantly and invests in a number of fields that have nothing to do with telephones or even telecommunications: magazine printing, cigarette carton packaging, banknotes, share certificates, deluxe printing, etc. What's more, the company is running operations not only in Canada, but in the United States and Australia.

The CRTC doesn't buy Bell's arguments. Its decision: for regulatory purposes, Tele-Direct's profits still have to appear in its parent company's financial statements, as they always have.

And what about Bell's other subsidiaries? The CRTC relies here on the principle of comprehensiveness. In simple terms, the organization feels that a portion of the revenues of all the group's subsidiaries, along with the investments Bell Canada is making in those companies, should be included in the calculations that determine subscribers' rates. But the body quickly realizes the task will be herculean. At this time, the Bell group numbers over ninety subsidiaries and associate companies. Studying their activities one by one to determine if any of them has an impact on subscribers' rates will require considerable time and resources, and almost certainly will set off interminable debates. The CRTC comes to the conclusion that, "le traitement réglementaire actuel des filiales et des entreprises associées n'est plus une méthode appropriée pour traiter les nombreux problèmes qui se posent dans ce domaine."[7] (The current regulatory treatment of the subsidiaries and associate companies was no longer an appropriate way to deal with the many issues that arose in this field.)

So the CRTC falls back on a simplified formula. It considers two groups: the first comprises activities that are part of telecommunications services – essentially Bell Canada and Tele-Direct; the second consists of all other activities. Only the first group is subject

7 CRTC, Decision 81-15.

to regulation. As for the second, it is reputed to make the parent company 1 per cent more than the authorized dividend rate – a rate set arbitrarily by the CRTC. In other words, if the actual amount paid to Bell by its subsidiaries is higher than the authorized rate, the excess has to be returned to subscribers, who will see their rates reduced. "And if the opposite happened?" asks a Bell executive at the CRTC hearing. If the subsidiaries make less than the authorized rate, will the company be justified in increasing subscribers' rates? The response is immediate: No, replies the CRTC's representative; Bell's shareholders have to pay the difference from their dividends. According to Jean de Grandpré, this decision defies all logic and is simply unacceptable.

> The regulatory authority was creating shareholders of a new kind – the subscribers – who would always be entitled to a share of the profits, never the deficits!

In the end, the CRTC will never manage to clearly decide between the Bell group activities that have to be regulated as public services (under the regime of the Bell Canada Act) and those that have to be left to the free market (under the regime of the Canada Business Corporations Act). But Jean de Grandpré himself will pull off this tour de force.

5

The BCE *Years (1983–89)*

A GLOBAL ADVENTURE

In 1983, Bell Canada Enterprises (BCE) becomes the parent company of Bell Canada, Northern Telecom, and some eighty other companies. The new organization, largely freed from regulatory constraints, can spread its wings internationally. Jean de Grandpré will bring the company to its zenith: the holding company has a stake not only in telecommunications, but in oil, gas, printing, and commercial real estate as well. In 1985, BCE leads Canadian industry; it is the first company in Canada to earn $1 billion in profits. BCE employs more than 100,000 people in subsidiaries in some thirty countries around the world. Here's a look back at a phenomenal episode in Canadian telecommunications history.

The decision to found BCE is almost a foregone conclusion. Jean de Grandpré thinks back to the circumstances that led him to orchestrate a spectacular coup that takes the century-old company to new heights.

> I was in London. The Bell regulatory officer called me to tell me about the CRTC's latest decision. The regulatory body was at it again: Bell had to continue to pay a portion of the profits earned for it by its subsidiaries and associated companies to the telephone subscribers (to the detriment of the shareholders), and, in particular, the profits from the lucrative contract with Saudi Arabia. I was shocked and appalled.

This last decision ratified by the Cabinet – Bell has appealed – on top of all the other ones that precede it, marks a point of no return. For Jean de Grandpré, it is now clear that the government is preventing Bell from flourishing.

> I told myself, that's the last time. From now on, Bell had to be shielded from any unfair decision that was against everyone's interests. I returned to my office. On a sheet of paper, I drew the outlines of the new corporate organization I had in mind – one that would enable me to ward off this death blow. I immediately sent it to our offices in Montréal: we had to see what its implications were for our thousands of shareholders.

The CEO doesn't know it yet, but he has allies. Even within the CRTC, the decision is not unanimous. At least one commissioner, Roy Faibish, records his dissent. Faibish chairs the subcommittee that had studied the question.

> "Such an incentive to conclude similar contracts [such as the contract with Saudi Arabia] abroad has major consequences. Firstly, insofar as such projects make a positive contribution to the revenue needs of the company, they lower the rate that subscribers of national telecommunications services must pay. On the other hand, the loss of such contracts will potentially lead to rate increases that would be higher than otherwise. The second impact is a wider scope; it includes public interest. I think that it is in the country's interest to encourage exports, particularly of technically advanced services and highly specialized equipment. The beneficial effects are doubled: such projects foster job creation; and they help improve the country's balance of payments."[1]

When the decision is made public, the entire financial community denounces it in unison. Jean de Grandpré does not wait for approval to act.

> As soon as I returned to the office, I discussed my project with Orland Tropea, who had made a career at Bell. Previously, he had been the regulatory officer and then vice president of administration. Most importantly of all, like me, he saw an international future for Bell. In short, he was

1 CRTC, internal document.

> the man everyone designated to follow me; he was my right hand, my alter ego. Stuart Spalding [V.P. finance] and Ken Howard [of Ogilvy Renault, now Norton Rose] took care of the finance part. Guy Houde, general counsel, obtained an amendment to the Companies Act so that companies incorporated by an act of Parliament had the same rights as chartered companies. All this to give Bell greater flexibility.

The plan is cut short. Before he officially announces it, de Grandpré shares his plan with his one-time political ally Ed Broadbent. He explains to him in detail why he has decided to found a new holding company. The NDP leader appreciates the effort and tells the Bell boss that it is the first time a company has done such a thing.

Fast-forward to June 1982, a few months later. The Bell CEO calls a major press conference to publicize a sweeping restructuring project. The new organization is built on the regulatory authority's recognition (CRTC decision of September 1981) that the Bell group carries on two types of businesses: the first are subject to regulation (telephone services and related activities), the second are left to the free market. But the line between them remains blurred and arbitrary. Jean de Grandpré makes things unequivocal: the Bell group, he announces, will now be reorganized according to the two types of activity recognized by the CRTC. The distinction is now quite clear.

And that is how BCE came into being. BCE will constitute the group's bridgehead, the new parent company, and Bell Canada (telephone services) will be a subsidiary. As for Tele-Direct, which has greatly diversified its activities since its creation in 1971, it will now be split in two: Tele-Direct (Canada) will take over the old company's multiple activities, except for the printing of the Bell Canada directories, and become a subsidiary of BCE; Tele-Direct (Publications) will publish those directories and be converted into a subsidiary of Bell Canada because that activity is a part of telephone services (by virtue of a previous decision by the CRTC). The same logic applies to Bell's participation in BNR and Telesat, which will also remain under Bell Canada's control. All of the other companies in the group, nearly eighty in total, will become subsidiaries of BCE.

The genius of the new organization is that it simplifies things. It rigorously separates what is regulated from what is not.

> Under Bell Canada [now a subsidiary of BCE], everything that is regulated; for the other companies of the group, everything that wasn't. This division faithfully followed the logic of the regulatory body … down to the last detail, however: the head of the holding escapes regulation and thereby finds himself free to act as he pleases in the financial arena.[2]

This freedom is essential for Jean de Grandpré. It gives the group the means to do business on a global scale.

> With a structure like that, we could better deal with competition in foreign markets. We were already in France, in Great Britain, in Saudi Arabia, but the strict regulation imposed upon us was an obstacle to our expansion. That was the foundation of the creation of BCE: it was about positioning ourselves as a major international player.

The creation of BCE makes a long-held desire of the group's leaders a reality: to cut Northern Telecom loose from Bell Canada's control and free it from regulation they have long considered abusive. The two companies are now on an equal footing, legally and administratively, and both are placed under the BCE umbrella. It won't stop them from maintaining their close ties on joint contracts, both internally and on foreign markets, this time as sister companies.

Everyone is taken by surprise by a move that has every appearance of a power grab. Yet the Restrictive Trade Practices Commission, which has been investigating relations between Bell and Northern for some ten years, doesn't dare rule against it. In a report it will submit only a few weeks after Jean de Grandpré's press conference, it refrains from issuing an opinion or a recommendation, proposing only that a public inquiry be held on the ramifications of the holding company's restructuring.

2 Rens, *Invisible Empire*, 47.

The battle

The federal communications minister steps into the fray. Francis Fox – the same lawyer who was once an intern at Tansey, de Grandpré & de Grandpré – is part of the Trudeau government, which seeks to shape the country's economy and especially its telecommunications development. Bell's reorganization will not go off without a hitch. Fox puts the question before the courts: Should the CRTC approve the project or not? Jean de Grandpré's reaction is immediate.

> If the courts were dealing with the matter, you had to expect a long delay (given the number of cases pending) – long enough, in any case, for the CRTC to get in on the act. And the next thing you know there would be another interminable debate. Everything threatened to collapse.

So he asks his lawyer brother, Louis-Philippe, to make a request, preferably to the Court of Appeal, so it can be heard as quickly as possible – which he obtains. The court immediately rules in his favour. Bell can proceed.

But the court's decision doesn't satisfy Francis Fox. The minister asks the CRTC to investigate anyway. He wants to know how the holding company's restructuring will affect regulation and, in particular, how it will affect subscribers' rates. The CRTC calls public hearings and in a few months issues its conclusion: it is in favour of the reorganization and recommends that the Bell Canada Act – the company's charter – be modified accordingly.

Yet despite all the opinions he has received, Francis Fox informs de Grandpré that he still opposes the project and that he will defend this position in Cabinet. The battle commences.

> I went to see the minister. I told him, "You were elected with a 5,000- or 6,000-majority vote. I have a million electors behind me, my employees, and my shareholders. And I am going to ask them to make themselves heard.

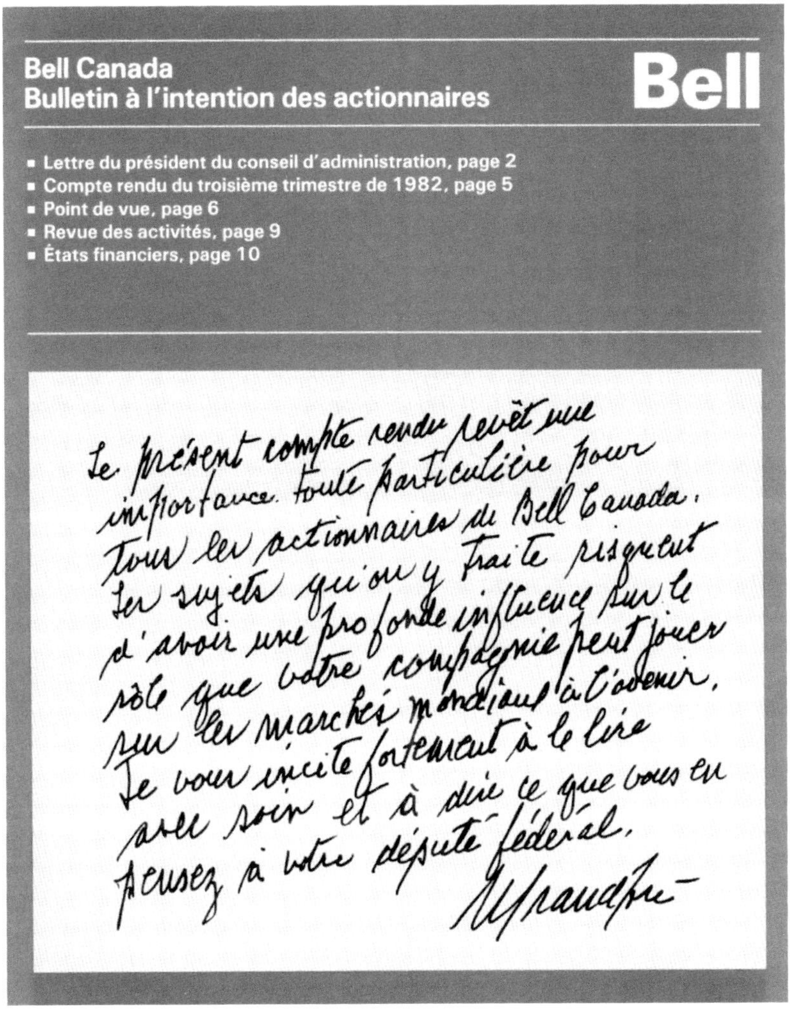

Bell Canada
Bulletin à l'intention des actionnaires

Bell

- Lettre du président du conseil d'administration, page 2
- Compte rendu du troisième trimestre de 1982, page 5
- Point de vue, page 6
- Revue des activités, page 9
- États financiers, page 10

Le présent compte rendu revêt une importance toute particulière pour tous les actionnaires de Bell Canada. Les sujets qu'on y traite risquent d'avoir une profonde influence sur le rôle que votre compagnie peut jouer sur les marchés mondiaux à l'avenir. Je vous incite fortement à le lire avec soin et à dire ce que vous en pensez à votre député fédéral.

And that is how the Bell CEO orchestrates a veritable coup. He handwrites a message on the page that opens the company's quarterly report ("the only time in Bell's history that a financial report will be published with a frontispiece handwritten by the president"). The text is concise:

> This report is particularly important for Bell Canada's stakeholders. The topics covered are likely to have a profound impact on the role that your company may play on the world

> markets in the future. I strongly encourage you to read it carefully and to share your opinions with your federal MP.
> – Jean de Grandpré

The tactic bears fruit, and federal MPs are deluged with letters. Jean de Grandpré's gamble pays off: the federal government declines to register its opposition. The Bell CEO can now proceed. But first he has to inform the shareholders. He never suspects that a final obstacle will stand in his path.

> Everything was settled. The government had accepted. I was going to convey the good news at my annual shareholders' meeting in Toronto. One of my representatives was in Ottawa and he was supposed to telephone me when the decision of the communications minister was made public. I was waiting for his call to officially announce the creation of BCE. I waited: 10 o'clock, 10:30, 10:45, 11 o'clock; still nothing. I was in a cold sweat. What if the government had changed its mind? Then, finally, the news arrived. The explanation for the delay? There was a fire drill that morning in the Communications Ministry building. What a relief.

In April 1983, just one year after Bell made its intentions clear, Bell Canada Enterprises is born. The name will be abbreviated to BCE sometime later, a decision the CEO will go along with. There is less confusion that way.

> The newspapers kept headlining their articles with the name "Bell." When we'd point this out to them, the news desk editors told us that our new name was too long. We solved the problem by adopting the name BCE.

Legislative amendments are needed to change the company's charter. Because things are never simple with telephony in Canada, the act respecting the reorganization of Bell Canada will be adopted only four years later, in 1987. Throughout that whole period, as he has done since his arrival at Bell, Jean de Grandpré has to answer questions, defend positions, and set out his arguments, but also soothe wounded egos and see others' points of view – especially when the person in question is a public figure. He always felt it was important to adopt this attitude.

> [If] you make a decision, you must be aware of the impact it would have on political leaders. They live in glasshouses. They must react very quickly, and you should also give them advance warning to allow them to think of their response to journalists.[3]

But the quibbling around the act's adoption will not prevent BCE from spreading its wings. And fast!

The Japanese odyssey

Jean de Grandpré is inextricably linked with Northern and has been since his arrival at Bell. The equipment manufacturer's success is close to his heart, and he spares no effort to support the subsidiary's development, putting his experience and network of relationships to good use. He has accompanied it on the Saudi adventure and will deliver another masterstroke with the Japanese odyssey in 1985.

The leaders of BCE and Northern believe the group needs a greater international presence. They envisage making it a world player. Japan and Great Britain are two important target markets, and both countries – especially Japan – will make all the difference in the years to come. The country is already investing over $30 billion U.S. per year in telecom equipment; it is the second-largest market in the world, after the United States. But entering the mysterious island is not an easy feat. The Japanese are very demanding, exacting clients.

> Northern [Telecom] was already selling equipment to the Japanese telecom companies. It was very lucrative for us. We knew the Japanese were very meticulous. Over the quality of the equipment, the complaints were rare, but a simple scratch on a package could make them unhappy. Strange, isn't it?

3 Campbell, "Adjusting to Win."

> But because the customer is always right, errors were not permitted. We had to satisfy them and, above all, show them we were interested in their market.

The CEO of BCE makes several back-and-forth trips to Japan and meets with bank managers, industrialists, and political figures. He tells them he wants to list his company's shares on the Tokyo Stock Exchange. At the time, the Japanese trading floor is considered virtually impenetrable to foreign groups. It is a considerable challenge. Jean de Grandpré overcomes it brilliantly. In November 1985, BCE becomes the first Canadian company to list its shares on the Tokyo Stock Exchange.

> More than 412,000 shares were traded in Tokyo on the very day trading opened. In total, the operation raised $300 million.

That feat is soon followed by another: Northern Telecom becomes the first foreign supplier of Nippon Telegraph and Telephone, one of the largest producers of telecommunications services in the world.

Full steam ahead

When BCE is created, the holding company is already on firm footing with the dozens of companies under its umbrella. But the group will experience accelerated growth with a number of major acquisitions. TransCanada PipeLines Limited (TCPL) is the first. Why would a telecommunications company want to get into the energy sector? de Grandpré explains:

> Our acquisitions always met the same requirement: they had to be complementary to telecommunications services, our raison d'être, our core business. That was the common thread guiding us when we created Tele-Direct in the early 1970s. And it was that same common thread behind our decision to take control of TCPL.

At this time, some find it strange that BCE is making a move into the energy sector, a field riddled with pitfalls. Not the holding company's former CEO:

> We were building an enormous network that had to cover a good part of the Canadian territory. It was important for us to have access to loose soil, acquired way back when, to bury pipelines. That was the royal road, if I may say so, for laying our lines. But we had to take certain precautions. I commissioned a study to verify if the heat given off by the pipeline had any impact on our wires. Once we made sure it was okay, we bought it.

BCE doesn't stop there. Sometime later, the holding company consolidates its position by acquiring Encor Energy Corporation. But BCE will not stay long in the energy sector. De Grandpré, and, later, his successor, will gradually separate the profitable activities (gas transportation) from the loss-making activities (exploration and extraction). The latter are sold first and the others follow. Are the transactions a success? In total, they make BCE $400 million.

Meanwhile Tele-Direct continues to grow by making several acquisitions. The company is still very profitable, but it is increasingly at odds with BCE's core activities. De Grandpré decides to sell it to Quebecor in 1987 (shortly before his departure). He makes a profit of some $10 million.

The year 1985 marks the introduction of cellular telephony. BCE starts out serving four cities: Toronto, Oshawa, Montréal, and Hamilton. But the network is developing rapidly, and new types of services are being set up under the Bell Mobility name. In 1987, BCE Mobile is created to integrate Bell Cellular, National Pagette, and National Mobile Radio Communications. It is an immediate success, and the company will grow exponentially.[4]

Another major objective is achieved in 1985: that year, BCE strikes pay dirt with $1 billion in profits. It's a record, a Canadian first.

4 Rens, *Invisible Empire*, 51.

> I am still proud of that success today. It was the first time in history that a Canadian company had obtained such a result. And the future looked bright. We were continuously strengthening our international presence. BCE's shares were being traded on the major stock exchanges in Great Britain, Switzerland, the United States, and soon in Japan. In short, we were where we were supposed to be.

In business, knowing how to profit from success always makes it easier to accept the inevitable defeats that come your way. The former CEO readily shares a wrong move the company made in real estate (Jean de Grandpré is nothing if not candid).

In the mid-1980s, Toronto is experiencing a real estate boom. To get in on the action, de Grandpré acquires a struggling Vancouver real estate company that will be renamed BCE Development (BCED). A short time after the transaction, the financial meltdown hits: the American mortgage funds crash and a spectacular fall in prices ensues; the real estate market collapses. BCED's buildings are not spared.

> BCE lost a great deal in the venture. Other companies hit by the crisis had swallowed up even greater cash outlays. But it's small consolation to say that we were not alone.

Thirty years later, de Grandpré has a clear view of events. According to him, the loss could have been avoided, or at least greatly mitigated, if he had followed the guidelines he had set for himself at the beginning: invest only in fields that are complementary to BCE's central activities.

> When the board of directors suggested we invest in real estate, I was first thinking of grouping all the buildings Bell and Northern Telecom occupied – there were many – together into one real estate company. The two companies would be paying their rent to this new entity. And I hesitated. I kept thinking of all the controls the CRTC had imposed on me over the years. Maybe I would be accused of giving the

> subsidiaries special treatment or of demanding too much from them. I just didn't want to get caught up in those discussions again. So I decided to first buy up real estate companies, in Canada and the United States, so I could have a basis for comparison. And then afterwards I could acquire the buildings Bell and Northern were in. I would rent them for the going rates so that I was beyond reproach. In short, I did things backwards. It was a mistake, yes.

And that is how Jean de Grandpré extricates himself from sixteen years of hearings and inquiries conducted by the regulatory authority and the Restrictive Trade Practices Commission. You can understand his reticence and his choices. Ultimately, the spectre of regulation will haunt the former CEO of BCE throughout his career. But de Grandpré never dwells long on past mistakes, no more than he does on past successes. He prefers to look to the future and to act. Again, he hammers home his catch phrase: "The worst decision is the one you don't make." Jean de Grandpré is not one to sit on the fence.

6

From Northern to Nortel
RISE AND FALL OF A TITAN

This is the story of a little company that will grow to become a colossal enterprise. From the early beginnings of Northern Electric, up to its meteoric rise as Nortel – a giant with feet of clay – it's a story with many twists and turns. At its height, Northern-Nortel counts for over a third of the total value of the Toronto Stock Exchange (TSE) 300 index. The company ranks as the ninth-largest company in the world and employs nearly 100,000 people on five continents. Jean de Grandpré is closely involved in Northern's rapid development, particularly beyond borders, in the 1970s and 1980s. When the CEO leaves the parent company BCE in 1989, the future looks bright for the subsidiary. A decade later, it is in rubble. A look back on the rise and fall of a titan.

In the beginning: the Canadian arm of AT&T

In 1895, the Bell Telephone Company of Canada creates a mechanical division under the name Northern Electric and Manufacturing Company. The company soon merges with another Bell division, Imperial Wire and Cable, to become Northern Electric Co. Ltd. The new company produces equipment for the Bell Canada network, but also a range of other goods – telephone bells, sleigh bells, the first gramophones manufactured in Canada, and more. In the first half of the twentieth century, the company also manufactures household appliances (toasters, electric stoves, washing machines), radios for the army, and electrical and radar equipment for communication systems.

Until the end of the 1950s, Northern Electric has access to the technical expertise and product designs of Western Electric, a division of AT&T, which holds shares in Northern Electric. In 1962, the last shares are sold to Bell Canada; Northern Electric becomes an exclusively owned subsidiary of Bell.

The 1970s–80s: the imprint of Jean de Grandpré and company

Northern's astonishing growth throughout the 1970s and 1980s is due to managers of the highest calibre, particularly Robert Scrivener, Walter Light, John C. Lobb, and Edmund B. Fitzgerald. These men knew how to capitalize on the synergy between Bell and Northern, focus on R&D, and invest in new markets – first and foremost the U.S. market. Jean de Grandpré is inextricably linked with Northern's success.

John C. Lobb, lawyer and former director of Crucible Steel, becomes president in 1971. He is recruited by Vernon Oswald ("Nick" to his friends) Marquez, Northern's CEO. Lobb, an American, opens up the U.S. market for Northern, a crucial step in its development, and sets up a subsidiary there. Scrivener and Light, who have made careers at Bell, decide to make the leap to Northern in 1973. Both understand how important the interaction between Bell and Northern is and organize their projects accordingly. The two companies will join forces to create the BNR laboratories. Bell's new charter – obtained less than three years earlier, thanks mainly to the legal virtuosity of Jean de Grandpré – makes the joint R&D venture between the two companies possible.

Keep in mind that up until the early 1960s, the equipment manufacturer is largely dependent on products designed in the United States. But thanks to the clear-sightedness and boldness of Bell's leaders, Northern soon makes giant strides in the highly competitive telecommunications technology market. An example of that growth: in 1964, only 1 per cent of its products are designed internally; by the mid-1970s, three quarters of them are. Northern will capitalize on its innovations, the digitization of the networks, the liberalization of the American market, and the internationalization of its activities to rise to the top of the industry.

A whole range of products – created in the BNR labs and manufactured and sold by Northern – will soon raise the company to the ranks of a global leader in its field. The SP-1 electronic switch, for instance, cost $90 million in R&D; in only a few years, it will earn more than $1 billion. Another product launched in the mid-1970s is also a hit: the Digital Multiplex System (DMS), known as Digital World, the first fully digital central office switches in the world.

In the mid-1970s, the U.S. division (Northern Telecom Inc.) begins forming ties with small operators that run networks mainly in rural areas. One after the other, these companies – and there are many – enter an investment cycle to acquire new switching equipment. They will be the first clients for the DMS-10, which will soon replace all the old electromechanical switches developed decades earlier.

At this time, Northern has twenty-four manufacturing plants in Canada and six in the United States. It also sets up a research laboratory in Palo Alto, establishing a presence for the company in Silicon Valley. In all, the multinational employs over 21,300 people, of whom 15,000 are in Canada, 4,000 in the United States, and some 2,300 in places as far afield as Turkey, Switzerland, Ireland, Singapore, and Malaysia.

In 1976, Northern Electric becomes Northern Telecom. The new name reflects the technological revolution underway.

In 1980, Jean de Grandpré and Walter Light recruit Edmund B. Fitzgerald to the team. The newcomer has been on the U.S.–Japan trade relations committee and has a good knowledge of Japan, enough so to sell Northern's products to the Japanese telecommunications institutions. Over the years, he will learn more about Japanese culture, which will earn him the Order of the Rising Sun, created in 1875 by Emperor Meiji. Around the same time, Walter Light, then CEO of Northern, asks Jean de Grandpré, who occupies the same position at Bell, to chair his board; de Grandpré agrees and occupies the position for two years. The synergy is assured.

In the early 1980s, Northern Telecom seriously contemplates the use of fibre optics as a solution to replace its copper transmission cables. That's how the Fibre World initiative will come to be. Interestingly, Northern Electric published a research report as early as 1966 – the first of its kind – on the use of fibre optic cables to carry information.

In the years that follow, Northern Telecom continues to internationalize. Jean de Grandpré participates in the adventure as a natural ally, then as chairman of the board for a few years, and finally as CEO of BCE, the holding company that owns Northern Telecom from 1983. With his skills as a diplomat and his extensive network of financiers, bankers, and business leaders, he is able to build partnerships in countries around the world. The Japanese odyssey in particular pushes Northern Telecom to new heights. The company is now able to assist the European Union and Asian countries in their network modernization programs. It deploys its technology everywhere; in 1983, with its DMS switches, it begins making major inroads into China. The following year, the company sets up its European headquarters in the United Kingdom, the first country in Europe to open its telecoms market to competition. Northern Telecom will take firm root in Europe.

In the United States, the authorities dismantle the Bell System, which until then is under AT&T's control. Nearly 90 per cent of the American market is now open to competition. Northern Telecom capitalizes on its technological advances to become one of the largest telecommunications equipment suppliers south of the border, where it soon controls nearly 45 per cent of the public switching market. The company has a huge head start over its main competitors and places Canada in first place in network digitization, a trend that will take over the entire world in the next two decades. Northern's strategy consists of targeting the most promising markets. To gain a foothold, it creates specialized laboratories (United States and France), opens divisions, and forms alliances with powerful local groups.

Northern's revenues provide an idea of just how much the company grows: from the time BCE was founded by Jean de Grandpré until the time he retires in 1989 they triple, from $2.7 billion to $8.2 billion.

The mistakes of the 1990s–2000s

Around the turn of the 1990s, Northern Telecom makes two choices that will decide its future. One is smart: the company develops global expertise in two technologies that will grow faster than anything else that decade – optical networks and wireless networks. And one is not: Northern does not take the rise of the Internet seriously and bets heavily instead on "the infostructure," its proprietary network rival to the Internet. We all know what happens next.

Poetic justice? In 1970, the company is one step ahead of everyone else with its Digital World initiative; this time it is taking the opposite path and puts itself at a serious disadvantage.

In 1995, Northern celebrates its centenary. Its leaders mark the occasion by changing the company's name, first to Nortel Networks Corporation, then to Nortel. The year 1995 also marks the beginning of the dotcom bubble. Over the next five years, investors will lose all sense of moderation, and will inject millions into innovative small businesses in an attempt to carve out a place for themselves in a booming sector. Nortel's leaders, who have taken note of the losing gamble they made earlier – to compete against the Internet – attempt to make up for lost time by acquiring companies, particularly young companies that have numerous patents but few products on the market. They pay dearly for the effort.

In 2000, BCE gets rid of the last shares it has in Nortel, which represent 37 per cent of the company's shares in circulation. The transfer considerably increases the number of transactions on the stock markets (Toronto and New York). In a few months, Nortel's stock price reaches a historic high: $124.50 on the TSE!

The company represents over 35 per cent of the value of the TSE 300 index. Any pension fund that bases its portfolio on the 300 index is dangerously exposed to any reversal in the company's fortunes. Two years later, the bubble bursts. The meltdown is total: Nortel stock is now worth no more than forty-seven cents, and investors lose some $400 billion.

A series of events follow that weaken the company even further: catastrophic financial statements, lawsuits for fraudulent accounting practices, loss of markets, and the effects of the 2008 financial crisis on the technology industry. Nortel cuts one activity after another. In January, the company files for bankruptcy protection. It is the largest corporate failure in Canadian history.

The last word

At the time of Jean de Grandpré's departure from BCE, no one thought the Northern division would lose its way and end up at a precipice. How does the former CEO explain the fall from grace? And what could have changed the course of this sad story?

> Numerous factors contributed to Nortel's downfall. But the starting point of the debacle was easy to identify: the appointment of Paul Stern as CEO. And yet Stern had been highly recommended on the board by everyone consulted.

Dr Stern (he insists people call him that) arrives at Northern Telecom in 1989 from the Ferrari Automobile Company, where he had been an executive director. His mission: to make Northern Telecom the world's leading telecommunications manufacturer by 2000.

> From the time he arrived, Stern started cutting everywhere, mainly in R&D. He claimed it would yield higher results at lower costs. It flew in the face of the philosophy that had pushed Northern to the forefront. The board of directors bought it for nearly three years. But when the directors learned that Stern's main concern was to increase the appreciation value of his options, they summoned him before the board. He was fired as soon as he walked in. But it was already too late.

Jean de Grandpré designates another major actor in the Nortel meltdown: John Roth. This talented engineer joined Northern Electric in 1969. He headed Nortel from 1997 to 2001. At the high point of the dotcom bubble, *Time* magazine described him as "the most successful businessman in modern Canadian history."

> Roth had worked wonders as general manager of Bell-Northern Research. But as director, it was another story. It was Roth who was responsible for the buying frenzy that pushed Nortel to the brink. He planned to transform Nortel,

> long a telecommunications equipment supplier, into a world brand identified with the Internet. In doing so, he turned his back on Nortel's history, the elements that had made it a success. When the dotcom bubble burst, Nortel went with it.

When Nortel's stock price on the TSE began to fall, John Roth denied all responsibility and put the blame on Canada's industrial policy, which, in his opinion, left companies poorly prepared for international competition.

Analysts could identify other factors behind the debacle, says de Grandpré, but the factors Roth identified played a crucial part.

7

MAN OF INFLUENCE, MAN OF THE WORLD

Leaving one's mark: an expression one might think is coined for Jean de Grandpré. A man of influence who is the living embodiment of the term. A great number of organizations, public institutions, and even governments will avail themselves of his expertise and sound judgment.

> I am not a solitary man. I am sociable, I like people and I am always ready to meet someone new, whatever title or position they have. That said, I did happen to personally know the presidents of CP, CN, Alcan, Stelco, and Seagram. The president of the Union Bank of Switzerland was also one of my friends. We'd often play golf together, in Switzerland and down south. I was also close to the president of Royal Bank. And even closer to the president of the Bank of Montreal and the director of TD Bank. I think you might say that, yes, I got to know quite a lot of people.

Friends, business acquaintances – Jean de Grandpré didn't have to wait for the Internet to build a network of contacts. It is a network as extensive as it is prestigious. "I could call up any one of the people of influence in Canada," he says. Unpretentiously, he qualifies the statement: "Or just about."

People skills, intelligence, good judgment, and immense experience – Jean de Grandpré has it all. It isn't surprising that his expertise is so highly sought after, as much by decision-makers in the political sphere as leaders of the business world, in Canada and abroad. Is Jean de Grandpré a man of influence? That's an understatement.

But he wants to make one thing clear.

> My career would have been very different if I had not crossed paths with influential people who had faith in me. I'm thinking most of all here about Robert Scrivener and Bill Hewlett, founder of Hewlett-Packard. I'm convinced: without a mentor to open the way for you, it's nearly impossible to really get ahead.

On the art of administration

The TD Bank, TransCanada PipeLines, Northern Telecom, Seagram, Stelco, Sun Life of Canada, DuPont – Jean de Grandpré has sat on numerous boards.

His international prestige is such that his voice is heard beyond borders, from the board of directors of the Conference Board of New York to the Chrysler Corporation of Detroit, whose destiny he helps to shape from up close. And yet, "At Chrysler, I had a very different influence from what was expected of me in the beginning."

It is one of his business acquaintances (John Coleman, vice president of Royal Bank) who suggests de Grandpré replace him on the boards of Chrysler Canada and Chrysler U.S.A.

> First, I had to get the authorization of the Bell board, which gave me the go-ahead. Because the vast majority of our automobile fleet came from Chrysler, having a vote in the company wouldn't be a bad thing.

Initially a member of Chrysler's compensation committee, de Grandpré succeeds Bill Hewlett as committee chairman. And he helps hire the new president, Lee Iacocca. At the time, Iacocca is a star in the industry who wins recognition at Ford for launching the legendary Mustang, an icon in automobile history. At Chrysler, the flamboyant Iacocca soon celebrates another feat: he literally saves the company, which is in dire financial straits, from bankruptcy.

> The directors, led by Iacocca, lobbied hard in Washington to obtain aid. Finally, the government agreed and lent Chrysler $1 billion. It would not lose out: the amount would be paid back to the U.S. [Department of the] Treasury three years

> later, and the company would post a profit. The mandatory presence on the board of Douglas Fraser, president of the United Auto Workers, a man known for his intelligence and honesty, largely contributed to the operation's success. I think the Caisse de dépôt et placement du Québec and Ottawa would have been well advised to have a similar requirement after having paid out billions of dollars to Bombardier.

Throughout this readjustment phase, Jean de Grandpré, as compensation committee chair, is in constant contact with Iacocca. He scrutinizes the salaries of Chrysler's leaders, including the salary of the president himself, to ensure financial resources are being managed properly.

> Iacocca would set an example: he would agree to receive a salary of one dollar per year with the proviso that he could acquire stock options. Smart move. His confidence in his ability to return the company to good health would prove highly lucrative for him in the long run.

Jean de Grandpré gradually becomes close with certain directors who share his management philosophy. With Owens-Illinois president Robert Lanigan and Boeing president Malcolm Stamper, he soon forms a dynamic trio, the equivalent of Lee Iacocca's inner circle.

> We were involved in every major decision and had a lot of influence. A lot. To the point of making others jealous.[1] Some directors complained that we were too big for our britches.

Yet it is this very trio that ends up pushing the president to retire.

> Near the end, Iacocca had become a megalomaniac, arrogant and full of himself. In short, unbearable and unmanageable. The work he had done at Chrysler was absolutely fabulous; no one could deny that. Unfortunately, he had ended up

1 Levin, *Behind the Wheel*, 302.

> forgetting two fundamental rules of management: respect your collaborators and never take credit for their success. When he left, Lanigan, Stamper, and I went to Switzerland to meet with Bob Eaton, president of GM Europe, to make him an offer: in 1992, Eaton became president of Chrysler. Two years later, having reached the legal age limit to sit on the board, I resigned.

Jean de Grandpré participates less enthusiastically on other company boards, including the board of DuPont U.S.

> When I became a member of the board of Seagram, the company had a major stake in DuPont U.S., which gave it the right to appoint members to that company's board. As I was already a member of the board of DuPont Canada, it kind of went without saying that I would sit on the U.S. board. And so I did. Except that the directors on this board, all very close or related to the DuPont family, took a dim view of the arrival of this "intruder" into their circle. I confess that the few years I sat there left me with no memory of having contributed in any way whatsoever.

After his departure from Bell, Jean de Grandpré chairs the boards of two other companies: Theratechnologies Inc., a Montréal-based biopharmaceutical company. And Metro One.

Metro One, a U.S. telecommunications company based in Oregon, offers specialized, mainly cell phone-related services to large U.S. companies such as AT&T, Nextel Communications, and Sprint. In 1994, the company looks for financing to expand its operations. Tim Timmins, the president, comes to Montréal to meet with potential investors. And then Jean de Grandpré steps into the picture.

> The project made sense to me. So I agreed to pitch it to some potential investors among my friends. And to invest money and time in it myself: basically, they asked me to become chairman of their board. I stayed there for five years.

The inflow of funds helps the company take off. At one point, its value exceeds $1 billion. But in 2003, Metro One, battered by the dotcom bubble, shuts down operations.

No doubt about it: Jean de Grandpré always wants to be part of the action.

> When I left BCE, I wasn't going to twiddle my thumbs and do nothing! When someone pitched something that appealed to me, I jumped in. Those boards, plus the chancellorship of McGill that I occupied for a few years, were enough to keep me in shape. And reading one book a week! I've been called super active. Well, it's possible …

Jean de Grandpré will have the opportunity to share his wide-ranging experience as a senior manager with a number of audiences. The most prestigious international institutions are knocking on his door.

Cambridge, Harvard, HEC, and the International Management Institute

In 1982, Jean de Grandpré gives a lecture on the evolution of business corporations to a select audience of judges, lawyers, and distinguished Cambridge University professors.

> My objective was to demonstrate that managing a small company was completely different from managing a big one. In the first case, the two or three founding partners manage the company. In the second, the board does not manage the company in any way. I told them, too, among other notions, that it was important to keep in mind that today a shareholder is not the owner of a company. They're an investor. An investor who can be very "volatile"; sometimes, they'll only be a shareholder in a company for a few minutes!

Around the same time, John McArthur, dean of the Harvard management faculty, invites Jean de Grandpré to be part of a working group alongside an IBM vice president and three high financiers from Boston. The question on the agenda: What's the best way to choose a CEO's successor?

> We determined three possible avenues. One, if the vice president is competent and still has a few years ahead of them, the solution goes without saying. Two, if the opposite is true, you have to set up a race in which three or four potential candidates can face off against each other. Three, you identify early on in the company – so you aren't caught off guard – a candidate who seems to have the profile you're looking for. Next, you give them responsibilities in various sectors of the company and see how they make out in each case. Finally, if none of these approaches works, you have to recruit from outside, keeping in mind that, even if you've taken all the precautions in the world, your choice could end up being excellent … or disastrous. Those are the risks of the trade.

The International Management Institute in Geneva also seeks out his knowledge. The institute's director, Bohdan Hawrylyshyn, a renowned economist and member of the Club of Rome, invites Jean de Grandpré to join his working group, which is mandated to structure a program intended for CEOs.

Many students from HEC Montréal are also able to benefit from his knowledge, especially regarding the role and workings of boards of directors.

> I first made clear that a board of directors is not the manager of the company. Its role is to provide the general direction of the company and ensure its performance in every area: finances; evaluation of executives, including the president; relationships with clients and governments; etc. It also has to make sure that replacements are available when senior managers go. The very composition of the board is paramount. In a big company, there is expertise. The board must, therefore, be made up of people who have complementary strengths, in management, finances, and

public administration, for instance. In a small company, it's different. The founder – who could be a discoverer, an experienced salesperson, sometimes a developer – very often has highly specialized experience. They have to surround themselves with the expertise they lack; their board of directors has to be able to give them support. And whatever the size of the company, you have to remember that all directors are not made from the same mould: one will be very vocal and express themselves readily in a meeting, while another, more discreet, will prefer to share their opinion one on one. Both modes of expression are equally valuable.

I varied my teaching formulas. Sometimes I gave a lecture, sometimes I sent out copies in advance of Bell's annual report from the previous year, and, based on the texts, I answered students' questions. This formula was the most interesting in my opinion because it was real and dynamic.

De Grandpré will later give this master class at the University of Alberta and Saint Mary's University in Halifax, which has a highly recognized administration course.

Your opinion, Mr de Grandpré

"My mission was very specific: to enlighten the board on the economic and political situation in Canada as I saw it."

That is how Jean de Grandpré describes the role he played on the advisory committees on international affairs of two powerful financial institutions in New York: Goldman Sachs & Company and the Chemical Bank.

The role meant I had to circulate in the Canadian political and financial milieus to get a sense of the issues of the day. I enjoyed this immensely. Advisers from many countries sat around the table with me. Each had their own brief to give. I remember that, at the Chemical Bank, the representative from the Philippines gave us a very relevant presentation on democracy: according to him, there could be no true democracy without a strong and educated middle class.

> Likewise at Goldman Sachs. U.S. General Haig, after having visited China and Bosnia, shared his impressions with us: he predicted that China would succeed in overcoming its difficulties because the country was not suffering from hunger. In Russia, on the other hand, he predicted a very dark period. The creation of collective farms had proved a disaster. I painted my own picture, the most complete and up to date possible, of the Canadian economic and political situation. Sometimes these presentations were followed by discussions on more general themes – our respective views of democracy, for example.

Jean de Grandpré puts his acumen to good use in many other decision-making bodies, including trips to London, accompanied by the Bell vice president of finance, to meet with bankers and investors.

> On my visits two or three times a year, I detailed every aspect of the situation in Canada to my contacts. I'd often be bombarded by questions when my presentation was over. These occasions were also the ideal time to talk about Bell, BCE, our results, projects on the drawing board, etc. So the information circulated in two directions. These discussions were very profitable and made perfect sense given BCE's international ambitions.

Back in Canada, his leader's insight is sought by governments from every party. Jean Chrétien, then minister of justice under the Liberal government, mandates him to carry out a study on judges' pay: "At the time, you might have three judges on the same bench receiving three very different net salaries!"

Prime Minister Pierre Elliott Trudeau then invites him to sit on a committee mandated to establish the overall salaries and compensation of deputy ministers and presidents of Crown corporations. It isn't the first time Pierre Trudeau will seek his judgment.

> In the mid-1960s, I often stayed over in Ottawa to present the amendments to Bell's act of incorporation. On these occasions, I saw Pierre quite often; he was minister of

> justice at the time. When the sitting prime minister Lester B. Pearson announced his decision to retire, Pierre called the hotel room to ask my wife, whom he had known for a long time, to let me know that he wanted to speak to me. So I went to meet him in Parliament. When question period was over, we walked up and down the corridor between the Chamber and the Senate for over an hour. The subject of our discussion? Pierre wanted my opinion on whether he should run for leader of the Liberal Party. I gave him every reason imaginable not to: the loss of his privacy he cherished so much, his lack of enthusiasm at meeting strangers, the endless handshakes at meetings, the coffee klatches, etc. He told me that he had too often criticized those who wrote, like him, but never had the courage to enter the fray themselves. His comrade-in-arms, Jean Marchand, would have run he added, but he was sick, so it was impossible for him to take the leap.[2] Anyway, Pierre consulted me, he listened to my dissuasive arguments, but it was clear, his decision was made.

Brian Mulroney, a Progressive Conservative prime minister this time, makes him chairman of the Advisory Council on Adjustment in 1988 to study the impact of the Canada-U.S. Free Trade Agreement. In the final report, de Grandpré will stress the importance of improvement through continuous training and education. These, he believes, are two essential conditions Canada has to meet to emerge from the effects of the treaty unscathed.

Municipal politicians also clamour for Jean de Grandpré's skills. In the early '90s, then-mayor of Montréal Pierre Bourque sets him a mission: to study the possibility of creating an organization that will promote the advantages for businesses of investing in and moving to Montréal.

> I organized a series of breakfasts with bankers and heads of financial institutions, universities, and research centres. After

2 Jean Marchand, Pierre Elliott Trudeau, and Gérard Pelletier formed a political trio nicknamed the "Three Wise Men," or in French, *les trois colombes* (the three doves) after their election on the Liberal slate. Like the symbols of peace they were named after, they were seen as messengers of reconciliation between francophones and anglophones.

> a few months, I was able to tell the mayor that the project was a go; what was about to become Montréal International was gradually taking shape. But I didn't want to put the structure in place all by myself. So I approached Guy Coulombe, ex-president of Hydro-Québec, director of the Sûreté du Québec, and senior public servant par excellence to take on the project. He didn't let me down.

Jean de Grandpré also exerts his influence on the Conference Board of Canada, which he is a member of for over fifteen years.

> It was an organization that deserved support. It brought people from every sector of industry around the same table, where they could exchange their points of view on the country's future.

But he doesn't just make himself heard within established structures. In 1976, Jean de Grandpré co-founds the Business Council on National Issues (BCNI) with Royal Bank CEO Rowland C. Frazee and Alcan CEO David Culver.

> The objective of this businesspersons' association was to examine the economic and financial problems that Canada faced and that ultimately ended up affecting us all in one way or another. Naturally, the idea wasn't to get everyone to come to an agreement on the possible solutions. It was more about managing to identify points of agreement, so that we could avoid fighting over it on the public stage – which, let's face it, is generally counterproductive.

The group also seeks to develop ongoing relationships with civil servants in strategic positions in government, so they can keep up to speed with policies in the works and prepare for their impact. To do this, he will hire Thomas d'Aquino, a highly reputable economist and public relations officer.

The BCNI is a group to be reckoned with: "These companies represented billions of dollars; in other words, the heart of Canadian finances and the Canadian economy." This is still the case. Now known as the Business Council of Canada, this grouping of some 150 member companies is recognized as one of the most important lobbies in the country.

Jean de Grandpré readily admits that holding a certain amount of power is satisfying: "Otherwise, it's impossible to accomplish anything. And having power is rather nice." Who could argue otherwise?

A PRAGMATIC MAN…

In the 1970s, I made the decision to centralize the small Bell offices scattered across the city. Having offices all over the place was very expensive for us. Everybody had to go downtown when they wanted to meet. The result was that a lot of time was wasted travelling. I first commissioned a study to find out exactly where the financial centre of Montréal was. The answer was the quadrilateral bounded by Atwater and Saint-Laurent (west to east) and Sherbrooke and Saint-Antoine (north to south). So I decided to build the Bell Tower on De la Gauchetière Street. I was very surprised when, at the end of the 2000s, Michael Sabia, then president of Bell, chose to move the heart of the company to Nuns' Island. Not only was it miles away from the financial centre, but it meant the employees had to spend an inordinate amount of time travelling from home to their place of work. And once they were on the island, they had to live in isolation, so much so that the place was ironically nicknamed "Bellcatraz," in reference to the famous isolated island prison of Alcatraz – which just goes to show you! Even today, that decision is a great mystery to me.

… WITH A TENDENCY TO DREAM

When I decided to construct the Bell Tower on De la Gauchetière Street, the real estate investment company Cadillac Fairview (where I sat as a director) approached me about a development project: to make McGill Street the "Grande-Allée" of Montréal. Valuable buildings, such as the CN headquarters, would be kept, while buildings of lower value would be replaced. The artery would end up on the Lachine Canal, around which deluxe condos would be built. Kind of a lovely dream. Québec City and Ottawa didn't give their support, so the project fizzled.

8

MAN OF COMPASSION

Jean de Grandpré, the high-flying manager, lives and breathes business and finance. But on the side, there is still a lot of living that goes on, with all the joy, pain, and satisfaction that come with it. De Grandpré has never lost sight of that.

There is Jean de Grandpré the man of action. And there is Jean de Grandpré the man of compassion. This giant of the business world has a comfortable existence, thanks to his talents, but he never forgets others or the part he can play in society.

Ask Jean de Grandpré if he is described as a philanthropist and he'll reply laconically, "You can call me that if you want." He is clearly too modest to care either way. But he will become irrepressible when he tells you how well he thinks of the Montreal Neurological Institute-Hospital, the Papillon Foundation for children with disabilities, and L'Amitient, three of the organizations that receive his support.

Thank you, Montreal Neurological Institute-Hospital

"It's no coincidence that I gave my support to the Montreal Neurological Institute-Hospital (Neuro). I was compelled to do so by personal circumstances."

At the age of twenty-nine, Louis-Philippe, Jean de Grandpré's older brother, contracts a serious illness that attacks his nervous system. As luck will have it, his surgeons are Drs Wilder Penfield and William Cone, then leaders in the field. Thanks to the care he receives from them at the Neuro, Louis-Philippe recovers. And despite the paralysis of his right side, he will go on to have an illustrious career that will take him to the Supreme Court of Canada.

But that isn't all: Claude Baillargeon, one of Jean de Grandpré's sons-in-law, married to his daughter Suzanne, bravely fights brain cancer that ultimately kills him. "When someone close to you is sick," says de Grandpré, "You start reading up on the disease, on the treatments available, and on the current research in the field."

Jean de Grandpré himself benefits from the institute's expertise after a serious back injury: "If I can play golf easily now, I owe it to the institute's experts." From 1971 to 1977, he also sits as chairman of the institute's board of directors.

For all of these reasons, Jean de Grandpré and his family won't hesitate to make a generous donation to the institute's Brain Tumour Research Centre in 2000 to build an ultramodern communications centre.

> Having worked all my life to advance communications, contributing to the creation of such a centre seemed right to me. And I was particularly happy to give it my name.

A telemedicine, distance learning, and teleconference system, the de Grandpré Communications Centre will be equipped with the latest advanced technology. The concept is designed to facilitate learning and discussion between practitioners and researchers in the field from all over the world. And it leads to a significant first: the possibility for doctors to be supported, virtually and in real time, by experts during an operation.

The centre is a high-tech training facility with a splendid design: a brilliant combination that will earn it a major international award, one in which it will beat out no less prestigious an institution than Princeton University.

Papillon Foundation for children with disabilities: Giving wings

We're in the early 1960s on a beautiful summer's day. The de Grandpré family is at their cottage in Lanaudière. All of a sudden, Suzanne, one of the daughters, is stung by a wasp. Her body reacts badly.

One minute passes, then another and another; if she is not treated urgently, she will die. There isn't even enough time to get her to the hospital in Joliette, only a few kilometres away. But, by a miracle, a nurse is working at a summer camp nearby, the camp run by the Papillon Foundation for children with disabilities. Suzanne is saved. The story could so easily have had a tragic ending. Jean de Grandpré will never forget it.

In 1997, the de Grandpré children want to offer their parents a present for their fiftieth wedding anniversary. Jean de Grandpré suggests one: a donation to the Papillon Foundation. The sum will make it possible to build a large family residence, fully equipped to accommodate parents who are worried about being so far away from their children.

The story doesn't end there. Fast-forward eighteen years later, in 2015, and there's Jean's son, Jean-François de Grandpré, biding his time in a garage waiting room while his car is being tuned up. On the wall in front of him is a poster listing all of the garage owner's commitments to children with disabilities. This is no coincidence, he thinks to himself. He speaks to the garage owner, Jean Duchesneau, who also happens to be the Papillon Foundation's CEO: "My family knows your organization very well. Have any projects underway?" It so happens they do: the camp facilities are in dire need of renovations.

In the days that follow, Jean de Grandpré visits the campsite with his son and Jean Duchesneau, who today remembers the scene very well: "He examined the building, riddled with mould, and said, 'You can't do anything with that. You have to tear it down and rebuild it. Call your architects; I'll take care of everything.' He had been there for barely thirty minutes."

Then, thanks to other donations, a brand-new pavilion is inaugurated in the summer of 2016. Four other buildings will follow: two more pavilions, a cafeteria, and a gymnasium tailored to the campers' needs, the only one of its kind in Canada. In short, the generosity of Jean de Grandpré and his family toward the Papillon Foundation will give the children and their parents an entirely revamped camp.

And, man of action that he is, Jean de Grandpré does not simply donate cash. He also invests his person and his time, by closely following the work progress, supervising the work site, and meeting with architects, engineers, and contractors. He sees to everything.

For the gymnasium, he is the stakeholder in the negotiations with the Government of Québec, which subsidizes the project. The often-nitpicking requirements of the government will unfortunately delay construction by several months and increase the projected costs, which tests the former CEO's patience. No doubt about it, regulatory authority and Jean de Grandpré never got along very well together. "Wherever I go, whatever I do, regulation stands in my way. It's my karma!"

The bond is strong between Camp Papillon and the philanthropist: "I often go there. Seeing the children enjoying these beautiful facilities makes me happy."

Honesty, generosity, discretion – these are the three words that come spontaneously to Jean Duchesneau's mind to describe the great donor to the foundation.

> His integrity goes without saying: Jean de Grandpré is a straight arrow. His generosity is immense. And his discretion is exemplary! Being in the spotlight was never something he relished. Some time ago, I wanted to pay tribute to him in front of all the members of the foundation. He refused. I insisted: "But Mr de Grandpré, it's you who will be at the centre of the event!" Flatly, he answered me, "That's exactly why I don't want to be there." For all these reasons, I have deep respect for that man.

L'Amitient: cultivating the art of helping

Supporting the Papillon Foundation is not the first thing Jean de Grandpré did to make lives better for people with disabilities. At the turn of the 1990s, he provided the funds needed to set up a home – called Maison de Grandpré – to accommodate the residents of L'Amitient and the people who take care of them. L'Amitient is an agricultural community near Saint-Jovite. Adults with behavioural problems or who present pervasive developmental disorders, such as autism, can flourish by working in the fields and developing their artistic talents. And, every autumn, you can buy as many fruits and vegetables there as you can works of art.

In 2018, to mark the extraordinary commitment of the de Grandpré family to the community, the Government of Québec awarded Jean de Grandpré the Medal of Honour of the National Assembly.

Love of family. Love, period.

Jean de Grandpré is first and foremost a man of compassion for his four children, his nine grandchildren, and his nine great-grandchildren from his marriage to Hélène Choquet in 1947.

More than a wife and mother, his wife will be his constant ally.

> Hélène was the daughter of Azarie Choquet and Liliane Chartrand, sister of none other than fiery union leader Michel Chartrand! Hélène had her teaching diploma and adored children. In the beginning, she worked in Maman Fonfon's kindergarten. Then she created her own network through which she taught the children of family friends, up until our marriage.
>
> I changed jobs a number of times. These changes sometimes came with a temporary reduction in income. That was the case when I left Brais and Campbell in 1949 to join Tansey, de Grandpré & de Grandpré. I remember that, to make up the shortfall in earnings, Hélène and I would spend many an evening translating new insurance policies issued by our clients, which provided us with some very welcome extra cash. That said, living with a limited budget never stopped my wife from creating a comfortable home where it was always pleasant to live. Thanks, too, to her sense of humour, her great generosity and her unquenchable optimism, she overcame all obstacles.
>
> Whenever there was a need, Hélène was always ready to step forward. I was often called away for work, sometimes for days, especially when I was travelling across Québec to acquire small telephone companies. I was even pretty much absent for an entire year when I was a lawyer for the Royal

Commission on Broadcasting in the 1950s. And to top it all off, that year, the kids contracted contagious disease after contagious disease. Hélène valiantly held down the fort. I can confirm without the slightest hesitation that my wife largely took responsibility for raising our four children. With flying colours, as their careers attest.

Hélène also possessed an inestimable quality in my eyes: discretion. My children would say, smiling, "Maman is a tomb." I've got just the anecdote to illustrate it: In 1972, Hélène and I were attending a reception given by Bell. The president, Robert Scrivener, sharing a dance with Hélène, confided to her that I was going to be taking over from him very soon. And, believe it or not, Hélène kept the secret until my appointment as president one year later! "If it had never happened, you would have been too disappointed," she simply told me.

I remember my discussions with her when I had to make crucial decisions. She had excellent judgment. So every time we had to appoint a new associate, I invited the candidate out to dinner to see them in another light. Hélène was always there by my side. For me, that was essential. When we got home, if she had the slightest doubt, she'd ask me one question: "Are you sure?" I knew then that I had to take time to think about it – really weigh the pros and cons.

My wife often travelled with me all over the world. When Bell was doing business in Saudi Arabia, for example, she met the wives of the employees, sometimes bringing them magazines from which she had patiently removed all images of bras, bikinis, and other clothing that were potentially offensive over there. At the souk, she covered herself, as was customary, respecting the adage "When in Rome, do as the Romans do."

Perfectly bilingual, refined, elegant, at ease in every environment, and with innate tact, Hélène proved to be the ideal spouse for an international CEO; without her, I never could have had this career. Her life took a dark turn, unfortunately. In the last eleven years of her life, my wife had vascular dementia. Fortunately, she was able to stay home

> with special care, surrounded by her children who visited her regularly. She kept her sense of humour till the end, even during the worst moments.
>
> Hélène was a remarkable woman. When she passed away, I changed.

Hélène and Jean have four children: Jean-François, a retired Superior Court judge; Lili, who held several management positions at the Bank of Montreal and at Mercer Management Consulting before opening her own management consulting firm; Suzanne, a graduate primary care nurse; and, finally, Louise, the youngest, who, after her business studies, teamed up with her husband to launch the travel agency Merit Travel Group, which is now the largest private agency in Canada.

> There is no doubt in my mind that our children largely owe their impressive careers to their mother's talent as a teacher. Thanks to Hélène, they all got through the delicate period of adolescence without a hitch and they all went to university. My work took up all my time and I was frequently on the road. I think, however, that I did manage to pass on a valuable legacy to my children: the importance of taking care of others.

Message heard. Louise de Grandpré recently opened a community kitchen in Fredericton, New Brunswick (where she did her studies). She is involved in the programs of the Canadian division of the charity foundation WaterAid in Africa, a continent she visits regularly. Apart from being a member of the advisory committee of the Neuro, Suzanne contributes annually to the institution's research fund. Jean-François was chair of United Way, and currently chairs the Foundation of Greater Montréal. Last but not least, Lili was a member of the McGill board of governors. Now she chairs the board of directors of the National Circus School in Montréal, sits on several boards of directors, including the board of the Orchestre symphonique de Montréal, and is actively involved in management mentorship.

In December 2018, the whole de Grandpré clan, including the patriarch's four children, nine grandchildren, and nine great-grandchildren, got together to celebrate Christmas a few days early. Jean de Grandpré was about to fly off to spend the winter months under the Florida sun with Pauline, his companion of several years. "Pauline and her husband were part of our circle of friends," says de Grandpré. "After the deaths of Hélène and Pauline's husband, we became close."

Jean de Grandpré speaks of a crazy love.

> Crazy in the sense of being totally free. At our age, we can experience this relationship solely for the fun of it, without constraint or responsibility of any kind. Except the responsibility of taking care of those who need help.

After a nice glass of wine as an aperitif, the couple shares their meals together. "It's always delicious. Pauline could easily have become a chef!" says de Grandpré. Shared meals, but separate apartments.

"Jean was born with a horseshoe around his neck," said his mother, Aline. Jean's life shows that she was absolutely right. Not only was Jean de Grandpré lucky in love – not once but twice – but he experienced the joy of living life to the fullest by doing what he always adored: in his case, his passion for business. You only have to listen to him to know that the flame is still burning. Bright.

CONCLUSION

At forty-five years of age, at the midpoint of his life, Jean de Grandpré had nearly everything a man could desire. Born to a wealthy family that had instilled in him humanist values and an exemplary work ethic, he had gone to the best schools and excelled. While still a young man, he had already formed an extensive network of acquaintances. Finally, he had settled into a career that brought him great satisfaction: de Grandpré was one of the most prominent lawyers in the city. And the icing on the cake? The fact that he shared his life with a woman he loved and admired and four brilliant children he cherished. Others would be satisfied to sail off into the sunset.

Not Jean de Grandpré. He was not a man to stay confined within borders, whatever their form: the borders of a quiet career, the borders of a highly regulated public service, the borders of a culture, a language, or even a country. Or the borders of just one industry when he entered the business world. De Grandpré was a proud man who never ceased to have ambition: for his family, for the company that hired him, for the holding company he created, for the many companies and institutions he has helped, for the causes he still supports today.

For de Grandpré, the first quality of a leader is to be visionary. And he was just that: when he was hired to loosen the regulatory straitjacket that hamstrung Bell's development; when he made

BCE a force to be reckoned with on five continents; and when he took a seat on all the decision-making forums that sought his expertise. The CEO of BCE was never the kind of manager whose horizon was limited to the next financial quarter, simply to satisfy the shareholders. The medium and the long terms were always his first references.

Jean de Grandpré is part of the vanguard of a new generation of Québecers – back then, you could count them on one hand – who carved out a place for themselves in the Canadian economy. And when he took the most prestigious job in the industry, he reached that economy's pinnacle, which prompted one admiring analyst to say, "Canada had Pierre Elliott Trudeau, Québec had René Levesque, and Bell, Jean de Grandpré."[1]

1 Mussio, *Becoming Bell*, 90.

SOURCES

Academie des grands montrealais. http://grandsmontrealais.ccmm.qc.ca/fr/48/. Accessed April 2019.

Advisory Council on Adjustment. *Adjusting to Win*. Ottawa: 1989.

Bantey, Bill. "Un homme pas compliqué." *L'actualité* 13 (1973): 18–54.

Bell Canada. "Bell félicite Albert Jean de Grandpré, administrateur fondateur et président émérite du Conseil de BCE Inc., pour le Prix de carrière 2013 du Conseil du patronat du Québec." https://www.newswire.ca/news-releases/bell-congratulates-a-jean-de-grandpre-founding-director-and-chairman-emeritus-of-bce-inc-for-the-quebec-employers-council-2013-prix-de-carriere-512310061.html. April 2019.

Campbell, Florence. "Adjusting to Win – An Interview with A. Jean de Grandpré." *Canadian Business Review* 16, no. 4 (Winter 1989): 8–15.

Canadian Encyclopedia. "Telephone." https://www.thecanadianencyclopedia.ca/fr/article/telephone. January 2019.

Canadian Radio-television and Telecommunications Commission, Decision 18-15.

– internal document

Chartrand, M. "Jean de Grandpré – Président Bell Canada." *Commerce* (November 1974): 44–50.

De Grandpré, Jean. Interviews, December 2018–April 2019.

Delorme, G.P. "La race des bâtisseurs." *Entreprendre* (June–July 1995): 8–11.

Duguay, N. "Quand un géant chute." *Ici RDI*. January 2013. https://ici.radio-canada.ca/nouvelle/423508/chronologie-nortel.

Filion, L.J. "Jean de Grandpré: comparaison entre les conseils d'administration des grandes entreprises et des PME." Document from *the École des HEC*. Montréal: c2002.

Levin, D.P. *Behind the Wheel at Chrysler. The Iacocca Legacy*. Houghton Mifflin Harcourt, 1995.

Mussio, L.B. *Becoming Bell: The Remarkable Story of a Canadian Enterprise.* Montréal: BCE Inc., 2005.

Rens, J.-G. *The Invisible Empire – A History of the Telecommunications Industry in Canada*. Québec: McGill-Queen's University Press, 2001.

Royal Commission on Broadcasting. *Report*, Vol. 1, Ottawa, 1957.

Surtees, L. *Pa Bell: A. Jean de Grandpré & the Meteoric Rise of Bell Canada Enterprises*. Toronto: Random House, 1992.

Techno-Science.net. https://www.techno-science.net/definition/3905.html. February 2019.

Université du Québec à Montréal. Bell Canada en Mots and en Images de 1970 à 2000. https://archipel.uqam.ca/3578/1/M11605.pdf. February 2019.

Vézina, R. "L'homme qui a changé Bell." *Les Affaires* (March 6 to 12, 2010): 28–32.